T0096144

SOME SIZES FIT ALL

ADVANCE PRAISE FOR THE BOOK

'*Some Sizes Fit All* is a very good reminder that businesses have certain things in common. Call it the core of managing an enterprise. This book is a very good roadmap, filled with numerous examples of what everyone interested in business needs to keep in mind, when managing the peaks and valleys facing all executives.'—Henry Kravis, co-founder, KKR

'An insider's playbook to managing a business—not theory but real practice. Akhil Gupta brings decades of knowledge and experience in explaining the critical elements to success—from understanding best practices to the critical importance of good governance. The breadth of his intellectual prowess, in great evidence in the book, has always been an inspiration to me and will educate the reader.'—Chip Kaye, CEO, Warburg Pincus

'*Some Sizes Fit All* is an invaluable read for all, but particularly for people who have not dealt or worked with Akhil. Akhil brings unique and invaluable perspectives to problem-solving and creating win-win outcomes. He is consistently ahead of the curve with fresh perspectives and amazing ideas. And then making them so simple in application. I strongly recommend the book.'—Chua Sock Koong, group CEO, Singtel

'Akhil clearly lays out the universal principles of good business and why they matter. No jargon, no snake oil, just simple advice for everyone looking to expand, refine or improve what they do. I have no hesitation in recommending this book to new managers and industry titans alike.'—Rajeev Suri, CEO, Nokia

'Most business books sound alike, normally just a bunch of the same words thrown together. *Some Sizes Fit All* is different! It is to the point and based on common sense. Akhil Gupta's experience as an extremely accomplished business leader shines through the text.'—Mats Granryd, director general, GSMA

'Akhil shares his incredible experience and expertise and codifies it in a very readable and relevant book. All too often, management texts only focus on the unique elements of success—and there have been many at Bharti. This book serves as a very helpful guide to the important foundations of most successful businesses.'—F. Chapman Taylor, partner, Capital International Inc.

'A pragmatic and insightful book on various facets of managing a business by one of the most proficient practitioners. Akhil has not only drawn upon his incredible personal experience, but also highlighted some of the best business practices prevalent in India. This book is highly recommended for beginners in business, and would be a great refresher for seasoned professionals.'—Rajiv Memani, India region chairman, emerging markets committee, Ernst & Young LLP

'A fascinating read, as indeed some sizes fit all. I believe the one size that fits all commercial enterprises across the planet is a constant reminder that society has permitted an enterprise to exist so as to meet a societal need. An enterprise that neglects this core belief will rapidly erode stakeholder value!'—Kalpana Morparia, chairman, South and South East Asia, J.P. Morgan

'Akhil Gupta's leadership and acumen has been instrumental in building Bharti's success. Just like the laws of nature, this book is a bold statement of his beliefs, and gives a new meaning to the term "management science" and is a must-read guide for entrepreneurs venturing into new areas.'—Kaku Nakhate, president and country head, Bank of America India

'I enjoyed each and every discussion I had with Akhil at Bharti as it was always thoughtful and mature. In the book, I loved both the profound ideas as well as the simplicity of the approach. On the whole, this book contains pragmatic tips for both entrepreneurs and professionals to build high-quality and successful businesses.'—Manoj Kohli, country head, Soft Bank India

SOME SIZES FIT ALL

AKHIL GUPTA

PORTFOLIO
PENGUIN

An imprint of Penguin Random House

PORTFOLIO

USA | Canada | UK | Ireland | Australia
New Zealand | India | South Africa | China

Portfolio is part of the Penguin Random House group of companies
whose addresses can be found at global.penguinrandomhouse.com

Published by Penguin Random House India Pvt. Ltd
7th Floor, Infinity Tower C, DLF Cyber City,
Gurgaon 122 002, Haryana, India

Penguin
Random House
India

First published in Portfolio by Penguin Random House India 2020

Copyright © Akhil Gupta 2020
Foreword copyright © Sunil Bharti Mittal 2020

All rights reserved

10 9 8 7 6 5 4 3 2 1

The views and opinions expressed in this book are the author's own and the facts
are as reported by him which have been verified to the extent possible, and the
publishers are not in any way liable for the same.

ISBN 9780670094141

Typeset in Sabon by Manipal Technologies Limited, Manipal
Printed at Replika Press Pvt. Ltd, India

This book is sold subject to the condition that it shall not, by way of trade
or otherwise, be lent, resold, hired out, or otherwise circulated without the
publisher's prior consent in any form of binding or cover other than that in
which it is published and without a similar condition including this condition
being imposed on the subsequent purchaser.

www.penguin.co.in

MIX
Paper from
responsible sources
FSC® C016779

Contents

Foreword

Some Sizes Fit All is an 'Akhil classic', and captures the essence of his approach towards simplifying complex problems and then applying his genius in resolving them. Having watched Akhil from close quarters, I can vouch that his hard work, passion, curiosity and brilliant mind makes for a potent combination. In feisty debates and disagreements around the table, Akhil usually prevails, given his tenacity for finding solutions. He is extremely quick-footed to assimilate any new data in real time, which he processes to make the outcome richer. Having the benefit of knowing his unique approach, I know he will inevitably drop a gem which helps to get to a better decision.

This book is a must-read for all those who find themselves stuck in the cobweb of complexities and patterns that they operate in. I know there are so many of us out there who will welcome this refreshing approach of the 'art of the possible'.

New Delhi   Sunil Bharti Mittal
March 2020

Preface

Throughout my career, one verdict I have repeatedly heard has been 'one size does not fit all'. This is stated even more forcefully every time an organization fails to replicate its past success in a new market. Innumerable gurus and business pundits have lent their weight to this dictum, arguing that every new situation or market or environment calls for a fresh approach to business and requires the unlearning of what one might have learnt elsewhere, even if that had met with great success.

While this statement may appear to be obvious, it is often quoted out of context. The fact is that certain fundamentals of business—irrespective of line of business, geography or scale—are universally applicable. The application of these fundamentals results in clear strategy; what can be different on a case-by-case basis are the tactical solutions, which depend on local circumstances, habits and practices.

This book is an attempt to discuss the fundamental pillars for any business anywhere, and hence the title: *Some Sizes Fit All*.

The greatest proof of this is Mother Nature herself. For instance, take human beings. Irrespective of where we are born, the fundamental architecture of all human beings is the same, comprising vital organs such as the heart, liver, kidneys, brain, eyes, ears, nose, nervous system, skeletal system and so on. Yet, people from different geographies or races look and behave distinctly in terms of colour, height, facial features, food habits, etc. A look at animals, birds, insects, plants and trees reaffirms this fact.

I hope that this book provides clarity of thought at apex levels of dealing with new markets and new situations by applying time-tested fundamentals based on common sense and business experience rather than fashion statements and complicated consulting assignments. Also, my apologies to the wise gurus who may find this a 'conflict of interest' and who, without doubt, will dismiss this as an attempt to oversimplify a very complicated world that companies and managements cannot and must not navigate on their own without guidance and direction from experts.

But then, that is precisely what I intend to do— simplify what has been turned into a complicated business environment by using the most potent tool of all, one that each one of us possesses: common sense.

One concept that I strongly believe in and which is therefore repeatedly mentioned in this book is simplification. A big litmus test for me on this would be whether all readers—irrespective of their levels of education, experience or expertise in functions and industries—find the book easy to read and simple to absorb. Keeping this in mind, I have divided it into three parts:

Part I	Fundamental pillars of management
Part II	General rules for some specific disciplines
Part III	Activities/norms that comprise the 'way of working' of an organization

Since some of my most satisfying years have been spent in contributing towards building a telecom company that started in one city in India and is today in eighteen countries, I have let examples from the telecom world creep in while discussing some fundamentals. However, these examples have been provided merely to clarify a point and are not to suggest that these fundamentals apply only to telecom. Every industry will have its equivalents, and I have attempted to point some of them out at appropriate places. I would urge readers to apply these to their respective lines of activities, and I have no doubt that they will find them as relevant as my colleagues and I found them for telecom.

My wonderful colleagues at Bharti who encouraged each other to think out of the box with great results have been my inspiration for writing this book. However, I am acutely aware that what I am attempting is to swim against the tide, and hence if I drown, it must be attributed only to my lack of skill or understanding and not to anyone else.

I have taken the liberty, while touching upon the basic principles, of giving my suggested approach regarding specific issues. By no means do I intend to suggest that a different view will be wrong. In fact, any view, even a diametrically opposite one, would be great, provided it is adopted by an organization keeping in mind its fundamental issues, is in line with the organization's DNA and basic agreed philosophy, and is based on logic.

I would like to acknowledge that many of my suggestions in this book are based on beliefs and a philosophy deeply influenced by Sunil Bharti Mittal, founder of Bharti Enterprises. Sunil has been a very close friend and guide in my journey at Bharti.

SOME SIZES FIT ALL

PART I

Fundamental Pillars of Management

Every business, irrespective of industry, size or geography, rests on some fundamental pillars of management. The success of any business, I believe, depends on how strong these pillars are.

1

Business Model

'A business model describes how your company creates, delivers and captures value.'

—*Steve Blank*

The first and foremost necessity for the success of any business is to decide what business or industry it would like to pursue. Within an agreed industry, there will invariably be several segments or options. Out of these, management will need to choose which ones it would like to pursue and which ones it would like to leave alone. This decision on what a business would like to do is called a 'business model' in management terms. As is explained in this chapter, a business model is needed to provide focus and direction to the management. In the absence of a clear model, the business is likely to falter as management will waste energy on irrelevant issues and matters.

Accordingly, I feel that the most important pillar for the success of any business is clarity on its business model.

The issues to be decided on when agreeing on the business model would include (but are not limited to) the following (for ease of understanding, examples are given for a few industries):

1. The line of activity

As mentioned above, almost all industries have multiple segments, referred to as 'lines of activity', which the management needs to carefully consider and choose from. In most cases, one would have to choose one or some of them as it may be neither necessary nor possible to pursue all possible lines.

Telecom: Possible lines of activity include mobile telephony, fixed line, national and international long distance, direct to home (DTH) television, enterprise business, data centres, very small aperture terminals (VSATs) or combinations thereof.

Automobiles: These include two-wheelers such as scooters and motorcycles, and four-wheelers such as cars, sport/suburban utility vehicles (SUVs), trucks, lorries and all-terrain vehicles (ATVs).

E-retail: The choices include a full inventory model, with sales through the enterprise's own platform, that is, own billing (like Amazon), or pure marketplace, that is, billing directly by merchant (Taobao model).

Financial services: The various lines here include banks (commercial banks, payment banks or small banks), insurance (life and general), non-banking financial companies (NBFCs), stock or debt broking and exchanges (equities, currency, commodities, debt, energy, etc.).

Hospitality: The primary line of business in this segment is hotels, but these are of different categories, such as five-star, four-star or lower, self-managed or as a franchise of hotel management companies (like Hilton, Marriott, Taj or Oberoi), or by way of bulk arrangements within existing hotels, as in the case of OYO Rooms.

Restaurants: The many options include fine dining, casual, multicuisine or specific cuisine, quick-serve restaurants such as McDonald's, only home delivery or both restaurant and home delivery, etc.

Tours and travel: The possibilities include tour operators, such as Cox & Kings, TUI, Kuoni, etc., and online airline and hotel bookings, such as MakeMyTrip, Trivago, Yatra, etc.

As these examples illustrate, all industries have multiple lines of activities available to choose from.

If we look around us, we will see that some of these models have disrupted or created new lines of activity within existing industries. For instance, OYO Rooms, which contracts rooms in existing hotels in bulk and then sells them under the OYO brand, has created an altogether new segment of hotels.

Similarly, Uber has to a very large extent disrupted taxi services across the world with its cheaper and more convenient offerings. In the medical world, online consultations and online monitoring of health parameters are redefining consulting practices and the diagnostic industry by eliminating the need for a patient to physically visit a doctor or a diagnostic lab, at least for routine or follow-up matters.

2. Geography

In addition to choosing a line of activity, it is important to identify the region in which the management would like to operate. This could be a city, a state, a country or several countries. It is important to keep in mind, however, that it would be near impossible for any business to cover the entire geography available. Even the biggest global companies such as Google and Facebook started within a limited geographical area and later extended their reach to global levels. The choice of geography would depend on the resources and ambitions of the management.

Indian telecom: Should the business be confined to a few states or should it be all-India/pan-India? Further, within states, should the business be confined to Tier One, Tier Two or Tier Three cities and towns, or should it cover the entire state?

Automobiles: Should distribution and after-sales services be provided only in Tier One cities or should they also be provided in Tier Two and Tier Three cities or should they be all-India? For example, Maruti is all-India, whereas Mercedes, Audi and BMW are in Tier One, Two and Three cities only.

E-commerce: Should the business cater to only Tier One, Two or Three cities, or should it penetrate small towns and rural areas, or a combination thereof?

3. Target customer

Even within a line of activity, it is possible to cater to different segments of customers. Companies need to carefully choose the segments of customers they wish to serve since the business strategy and required actions will depend upon this. For instance, catering to a niche or high-end segment would involve a very different approach, resourcing and pricing as compared to a mass-based offering. This applies to almost every industry. A niche approach would require high quality and high prices while a mass approach would require good quality at affordable prices. The business models for each of the two segments are diametrically opposite. For the niche segment, the model would entail 'high per-unit margins but low volumes' while for the mass segment it would mean 'low per-unit margins but high volumes'.

The following are some examples of customer segment options within various industries.

Telecom

- If opting for a niche market, the business would target customers with an average revenue per user (ARPU) above a certain threshold per month. For example, wireline broadband customers with a minimum tariff plan of, say, Rs 500 per month.
- If aiming for the mass market, the business would target customers with low ARPUs only—say below

Rs 70–80 per month. Telenor and Videocon are examples of this approach.

- The business could also opt for a combination of niche and mass market, as done by Airtel, Vodafone Idea and Jio.

Automobiles

- Targeting the mass market would entail focusing on entry-level vehicles, as done by Maruti, Hero, Bajaj and Hyundai.
- The niche or ultra-luxury segment would entail offering cars above Rs 20 lakh or motorcycles above Rs 60,000. Examples include Mercedes Benz, BMW and Audi for cars, and Royal Enfield and Harley Davidson for motorcycles.
- Between the mass market and the niche lies the mid-segment, that is, cars between Rs 6 lakh and Rs 20 lakh, as offered by Chevrolet, Maruti, Toyota and Nissan, among others.
- A business can also target a combination of the above, as in the case of Maruti, Chevrolet and Hyundai.

E-commerce

- The business can target the mass market and offer all products, as done by Amazon and Flipkart.
- A slight variation would be targeting the mass market but offering limited products, as in the case of Snapdeal.
- At the other end of the spectrum is the niche market approach, adopted by Jabong and Myntra.

4. Sequencing and pace of expansion

If multiple choices exist in any of the parameters above, it would be prudent to decide on sequencing and priorities and the milestones/time period for the introduction of specific products/services or specific geographies.

For instance, if a telecom operator wishes to establish an all-India presence, it must decide where it will set up operations first—big cities or mid-size cities—and the pace at which it will expand and where. Normally, companies adopt a 'ripple effect' approach, wherein they start from a focal point and thereafter keep expanding their area of influence or 'circle'.

For instance, if Karnataka is the chosen state, the focal point could be Bengaluru. The network expansion plan could look as under:

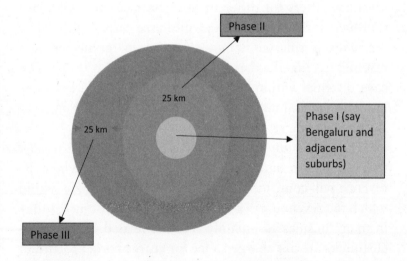

The ripple effect approach is adopted as it is neither possible nor desirable to spread limited resources too thin by covering the entire desired geography at the very beginning or in one go. It is prudent to expand once enough experience has been gained so that successes can be focused on and mistakes can be avoided.

5. Revenue and profitability model and timing

The Cambridge Dictionary defines the term 'business' as 'the activity of buying and selling goods and services'. Since the buying of goods and services requires payment or expenditure, the selling of goods and services would have to entail receipts. Such a receipt is known as 'revenue'. The prime purpose of a business is to earn more revenue than its expenditure, whereby it earns a profit. Conversely, if expenditure is more than revenue, it shall experience a loss.

The time frame within which a business starts to earn revenues differs for different businesses. Some could earn revenues sufficient to give a profit in the early stages, while for many businesses it may take time to garner enough revenue to exceed expenditure. Traditional businesses can earn revenues within a shorter time period, whereas some modern-day online businesses can take much longer to start generating revenues.

Thus, it is important to have a clear revenue model, that is, a proper understanding of how and from where the revenue will come in, and also to have a time frame within which the revenue will start coming in. For instance, today in many businesses—mainly Internet-related businesses—customers are not charged a fee for years in order to attract more and more customers. However, there must be a clear realization as to when, or after reaching what kind of customer base, the business will start earning revenue.

The biggest and most prominent examples are Internet companies such as Google.

Google, despite providing some of the most brilliant and finest services to its customers, for example, Google Search and Google Maps, does not charge its customers. However, it has had a very clear revenue model from day one, namely, advertising revenue. The same goes for other successful companies such as YouTube, Facebook and Twitter.

Companies that cannot demonstrate a revenue and profitability model do go out of favour sooner or later.

Any business where revenue and/or profitability cannot be convincingly demonstrated over the foreseeable future, say five to seven years at the most, is likely to fail or run out of money at some point.

Lately, some proponents of 'new school' businesses, which are primarily Internet-based, have started believing that such businesses can be permanently run without revenues and profits. This is based on the assumption that funding from external investors will be available permanently based merely on customer counts and transaction volumes. In their view, businesses based on traditional models of revenue and profits are 'old school' and are not keeping pace with the times. Unfortunately, the stock markets too have started reflecting this sentiment when it comes to valuations of new-school versus old-school businesses. Valuations for traditional or old-school businesses believing in revenue, profits, cash flows and dividends are generally low these days.

However, it is my belief that, ultimately, the old school will be the one that remains standing long after several new schools have collapsed. In fact, as I move towards completion of this book, a major shift in this regard is already happening with collapse of valuations at WeWork and Uber due to continuing losses and cash burn. This has led even Masayoshi Son, CEO of Soft Bank and Vision Fund, who till recently advocated, promoted and invested only in businesses which could show big growth, even at the cost of huge cash burns and losses, to shift his belief and start recognizing the importance of profitability.

It is not important where the revenue comes from. Perhaps the best revenue model is where revenue comes from someone other than the company's own customers, as in the case of Google and credit and debit card companies, which are paid by advertisers and merchants (and not their customers), respectively.

6. Clarity of objective

Many organizations take pride in claiming that their mission is to make the world a better place to live for the common man. This is a fine objective, but I feel that every business needs to be clear as to what its main goal is—is it philanthropy or running a profitable business?

The right answer to my mind is that the objective should be to run a successful and profitable business with rapid scale-up using ethical means. If in the process the business embarks on a journey that enriches human life, such as in the case of manufacturing non-polluting automobiles, generating renewable energy, etc., even better. However, it is a fallacy that industries which supposedly do not make this world a better place are no good. Take, for example, the gambling industry. On the face of it, gambling is a terrible thing, but the industry does provide huge development opportunities for entire regions, as demonstrated by Las Vegas and Macau. Both cities boast massive inflows of tourists and hence a booming hospitality industry. This provides employment to a large number of people, thereby making this world a better place to live for them and their families. The gambling industry also provides huge revenues to the exchequer, which again helps the common man lead a better life.

I feel it is imperative for all organizations and employees to understand that they can only fulfil their philanthropic aims by being profitable. Bankrupt companies cannot indulge in philanthropy.

It is my belief that every business inherently performs a fundamental philanthropic activity, and that is providing employment to people, both direct and indirect. To me, this is far superior to any charity because unlike the recipient of charity, the employee earning a livelihood is able to take care of his or her family with pride and dignity rather than through the mercy of someone else's handouts.

7. Revisit the business model at regular intervals

It is important for every company to revisit and review all aspects of its business model at regular intervals. These intervals can be time-based, say, annually, or can depend on specific events, such as regulatory changes, new technological innovations, the emergence of new markets, etc.

As the world changes at a fast pace, this exercise attains increasing importance and thus needs to be institutionalized.

I believe that all the principles discussed above are applicable to all kinds of businesses without exception—

whether they are in manufacturing, services, infrastructure, logistics, or are combinations thereof. Applying these to a business in a methodical manner will result in clarity regarding the ideal business model for a particular enterprise. By the way, I am certain that subconsciously, people do think of some or all of these factors in a random and unstructured manner. The difference between such an unstructured exercise and a structured thought process is the difference between chaos/confusion and order/clarity.

2

Business Delivery Model

Once an organization finalizes its business model, the next step is to decide on a business delivery model.

Business delivery, as the term suggests, is the way an organization decides to deliver or execute its business model.

Two fundamental issues that can form the core of delivery options are:

1. Asset-Light or Asset-Heavy
2. People-Light or People-Heavy

A company choosing an asset-light model would choose to lease properties and assets rather than own them. Accordingly, it would replace depreciation on assets and interest on investment with recurring lease charges. This decision, though seemingly simple, generally involves taking into account a complex set of factors—financial and emotional. Typically, an organization will have two camps—one that prefers to own assets and thus not be bound by any restrictions that may come with leasing. For instance, in an owned building, one can alter or add things over time while in a leased building, such a decision would need the landlord's approval and finalizing fresh terms.

The other camp is the one that believes in putting the least amount of capital possible into the business to maximize return on capital employed by taking advantage of lower lease costs versus overall cost to the company if an asset were owned by it. This could be due to better economies of scale in the hands of the lessor, his/her specialization in lowering running costs or better sweating of an asset by sharing it and having maximum capacity utilization.

Another area that often sees division is the preference for a people-light or people-heavy model. A lot of companies take pride in claiming that they employ a large number of people while others are proud of claiming that they run a large business with very few people on their rolls, while of course still claiming that they provide direct and indirect employment to a large number of people.

The above decisions are dependent on two major arguments. One, that by outsourcing certain activities the company loses control over quality and expertise as the outsourced partner will offer these to the competition as well. Two, that when it comes to a decision regarding the ownership of assets, often, a large company will have the advantage of negotiating a better price for purchasing assets than a smaller-sized company, which would purchase such assets and then lease them to the larger-sized company. This could lead to adverse lease terms vis-à-vis owning such assets.

Guidelines for outsourcing or insourcing

One dilemma all organizations face is deciding which activities should be outsourced, that is, sourced from an entity or entities outside the company. The most common example of outsourcing for many industries is handling of customers' calls and complaints by specialist business process outsourcing (BPO) companies (some prominent BPOs in India are Genpact, Wipro and IBM Daksh). Similarly, some highly specialized activities such as the processing of insurance claims are also routinely outsourced to knowledge process outsourcing (KPO) companies in India. Being an important decision, there must be sound reasoning behind such decision-making.

After a lot of deliberations and brainstorming, we at Airtel identified three questions to help determine whether an activity should be outsourced or insourced:

1. Who has the better domain knowledge of the subject/ activity—the company or the external agency?
2. Who can attract better human resources for the activity?
3. Who has better economies of scale (on account of bigger volume handled) for the activity under consideration?

Only if the answers to all three questions are in favour of an outsider or if the answers to two are in favour of an outsider with the third being split equally between self and outsider should the activity be outsourced.

Let us test the application of these three questions to determine the capabilities of a company like Airtel versus those of an outside agency with regard to two very diverse activities—information technology (IT) and housekeeping.

IT (say, IBM versus Airtel) versus Housekeeping

The answers to the three key questions for IT are as under:

1. IBM has significantly better domain knowledge on all aspects of IT vis-à-vis Airtel.
2. IBM has more talent and expertise in the realm of IT than Airtel.
3. Since IBM operates globally on a massive scale, they enjoy better economies of scale than Airtel.

Now, let us test these same questions for a somewhat mundane and low-skill-level activity like housekeeping, that is, maintenance and cleaning of premises, applying them to a specialized housekeeping agency (for example, Knight Frank) versus a large company like Airtel.

1. Airtel, or for that matter any large company, would invariably fall short of domain knowledge on cleaning and maintenance services as compared to the agency.
2. The agency will be better placed than the company to attract and train people required for housekeeping.
3. The agency will have a much lower cost structure than the company due to its scale and specialization in this particular activity.

In fact, these questions can be applied to any activity, irrespective of level of technical complexity, and the answers will always lead to the correct decision.

However, it is important to remember that only an activity or job can be outsourced and not the responsibility. The end responsibility must still lie within the company, irrespective of whether the activity is outsourced or insourced. This will ensure the accountability of the people entrusted with supervising the outsourced partner.

Furthermore, an organization must outsource only activities and never the thinking. Companies that outsource decision-making on strategy will invariably fail due to lack of ownership and alignment. One could outsource preparatory work and even invite suggestions from consultants, but the final decision based on debate and thinking must be made by the organization.

Airtel experience

Perhaps the telecom industry in India is a prime example of this debate on outsourcing versus insourcing, with Airtel having been at the centre stage. We tried to base our decisions on whether to outsource certain activities on the principles discussed above. Below are some examples.

Outsourcing IT

At an early stage of Airtel's existence, when we went for a massive expansion in our operations in 2003 by acquiring mobile licences for all India circles (all states of India), a major problem faced was with regard to investments and operational aspects related to IT deployed. IT is at the core of operations of any telecom operator as it connects the telecom network elements to customers and trade by way of customer billing, customer service, data analysis, billing to trade intermediaries and core accounting. We realized two startling facts: first, good IT professionals often did not want to join telecom companies, and that too a struggling small company like Airtel with big ambitions, whose future was, to say the least, challenging. They preferred to work for big IT companies such as IBM, HP, Cisco, Infosys, TCS or Wipro. That left a big gap on the capability front within Airtel.

Second, in the IT world, a long-term solution required a company to make large investments in hardware and software upfront, and the equipment deployed became obsolete at an alarmingly fast pace, requiring frequent replacement. Both of these factors were disturbing to us at Airtel. One, we did not have the capital to make the large upfront investments required for ideal IT solutions and thus invariably settled for suboptimal solutions requiring smaller investments. Two, we were not used to seeing seemingly perfectly functioning hardware/software being categorized within a year or two as needing replacement because, for instance, the new version of Oracle or the billing software could not work on the existing servers. Particularly painful was a conversation I once had with the head of the IT department about the future of some servers that we had bought a few years before at a cost of several million dollars. He told me that although the servers were now obsolete for our needs, we would not dump them but would use them as email servers instead. That to me was too much to digest—that such expensive servers would now be used for such a rudimentary activity as email management.

The two problems concerning talent and capital investments led us to take the bold, transformational and innovative decision to outsource Airtel's entire IT operations to IBM (of course, this was done after a formal process of issuing a request for proposals from major

Indian and global IT companies). What was innovative and bold in this was that unlike the outsourcing of other IT activities that entail the running and maintenance of day-to-day operations—services that were common and were offered by many reputed companies like Infosys, TCS, Wipro and IBM—our model entailed the total and comprehensive outsourcing of IT activities involving hardware, software and services to IBM. The contract was complex as we had to safeguard Airtel's interests vis-à-vis the freedom to choose best in class hardware and software and be assured of world-class service-level agreements (SLAs), which clearly specified agreed deliverables for each element of IT deployment along with agreed penalties and rewards for under-achievements and over-achievements vis-à-vis the agreed levels of respective performances. On the other hand, IBM had to safeguard itself financially as it was expected to make upfront investments but was to be paid a percentage of revenue over the next ten years. (These peculiarities are further discussed in the section on clarity on compensation later in this chapter.)

Outsourcing network operations and maintenance

Similar issues, particularly regarding manpower, arose when it came to the planning, procurement, deployment, maintenance and upgrade of different elements required for telecom networks. A mobile or cellular network consists of hundreds of elements, the prominent ones being the switch, radios, antenna to receive and send signals, microwaves and optic fibre to transmit traffic between the telecom tower and the master switching centre (MSC).

At the time, network engineers preferred to work for companies such as Ericsson, Nokia, Alcatel or Motorola, which were big global equipment suppliers to telecom operators and were also our vendors. Thus, for a long time, we struggled with the problem of not being able to attract the required human resources, resulting in inadequate internal expertise to conduct the above-mentioned functions (which come under the umbrella of network operations and services). After a lot of deliberations, we at Airtel decided that for our situation, the best option was to entrust the equipment manufacturers themselves with all aspects related to network operations and services. One major concern was whether we would become overly dependent on such vendors. Two factors that made us take this risk were that firstly, the vendors were global giants of repute—such as Ericsson, Nokia, Motorola and Alcatel— and thus the risk of being taken for a ride was remote.

Secondly, with such outsourcing to vendors themselves, we were able to pin responsibility for network performance on them. This was a major factor for us as we could ill afford the prospect of finger-pointing amongst persons responsible for the different tasks related to network operations and quality, with some aspects being handled internally by our employees and the rest by the vendor, in the event of network failures or poor quality.

However, as stated earlier, the overall responsibility for network performance still rested with us since our customers would hold us accountable if the network quality was not satisfactory. Thus, clear responsibilities were assigned to individuals within our company to supervise, monitor and analyse the key indicators for network performance on the one hand and take prompt corrective actions in consultation with the vendor on the other. In the event of an unsatisfactory response from the vendor, the matter was to be escalated to higher levels.

A first-of-its-kind arrangement—not just for our company but for the telecom industry itself globally— that was part of this outsourcing was the mode of compensation and payment to the vendor for the active network equipment (that is, the electronic equipment that made functioning of the telecom network possible) purchased by us.

Decisions of the nature mentioned above need to be taken in every industry and every organization. Our experience in the telecom industry is perhaps an example of the various factors that can be considered when taking these decisions.

Outsourcing passive infrastructure

As mentioned earlier, telecom infrastructure can be broadly classified into the following categories:

1. Active or electronic elements, for example, radios, MSC, base stations (BTSs) and base station controllers (BSCs) and antennas, which are at the core of receiving and sending telecom signals from and to customers.
2. IT network and infrastructure, which comprises hardware such as servers, computers, laptops, etc., and the software that operates on such hardware.
3. Transmission elements, which transmit the traffic generated on the network, for example, microwaves that transmit wireless signals and the optic fibre network that transmits via wire.

4. Passive infrastructure, for example, telecom towers on which active network equipment is placed, which, besides the steel structure, has the power supply system to source power from various sources such as the grid, batteries installed at site, diesel-generating sets or solar-generating equipment installed to generate power in the event of non-availability of grid supply from the electricity board and from batteries installed.

Ever since the advent of telecom, it was believed that towers represented a big competitive advantage as a new entrant took time, capital and effort to replicate that infrastructure. It is indeed true that not sharing that infrastructure gave a competitive edge to the incumbent for the period that the challenger took to replicate it—usually six months to a year.

We at Airtel also followed this industry norm for the first decade of our existence. Indeed, where we were the leader, we were able to delay replication by a new competitor by about six to twelve months by not sharing our passive infrastructure with them. Vice versa, our entry too was delayed by similar periods where we were the challengers as the incumbent refused to share its infrastructure with us.

However, that was where the competitive advantage ended. The result of this practice was that the industry saw four or five towers erected within fifty metres of each other by different operators whereas only one would have sufficed. We also realized that we had forced each other to spend huge amounts of capital, paying steel and cement companies, diesel generator manufacturers, battery manufacturers, etc. as well as replicating operating expenditure (opex) by way of maintenance of equipment, rent to landlords, personnel expenses, IT, etc.

It became clear that this redundant capital expenditure (capex) and opex on the towers could be avoided if the operators shared one tower and placed their respective active equipment thereon. To address this wasteful industry experience, in 2007 when Airtel only had some 50,000 towers (as against close to 2,00,000 today), we decided to demerge our tower infrastructure (not active infrastructure) into a separate company, which was initially a wholly owned subsidiary. The mandate was that the new management should run this company as an independent company and share the infrastructure with all operators on a non-discriminatory basis in terms of charges as well as SLAs. A master service agreement was created, giving standard rates for ground-based towers and rooftop towers with location premiums for difficult or expensive geographies with specified volume discounts and SLAs. A unique and innovative feature was that as the same tower was shared by several operators, the rates came down for all operators by way of sharing the benefits that accrued to the tower company, thereby resulting in a win-win situation for the tower company as well as the customer. The first occupant did not even have to apply for a lower rate—it automatically got it the moment another occupant came in.

We subsequently invited Vodafone to also demerge their towers into this company, followed by Idea, which became the third party in this joint venture. This practice not only reduced opex costs for all but also avoided capex for telecom companies (passive infrastructure accounted for approximately 60 per cent of the total capex of a telecom company at that time). This company, which has now been replicated by Chinese telecom companies, is named 'Indus Towers', with no one operator holding a majority. This became a classic case of collaborating on the back end while fiercely competing on the market front. With more and more telecom operators across the globe now separating their tower infrastructure into specialized tower companies, this is becoming a global practice, and accordingly the number of sceptics who still believe that sharing of infrastructure results in a competitive disadvantage is fast shrinking. While there existed tower companies that had set up their own towers and leased them out to telecom operators (for example, American Tower Company and Crown Castle), India emerged as the pioneer and trendsetter in terms of the operators divesting their towers to tower companies or forming tower companies separately as a joint venture with competitors. The latter, that is, combining towers with competitors under an independent and non-discriminatory tower company, was certainly unimaginable prior to the formation of Indus Towers.

All these outsourcing arrangements have been subjects of case studies at Harvard Business School for MBA and AMP (advanced management programme) classes due to the underlying innovative and pioneering initiative and thinking.

Clearly, the decision to outsource certain activities, particularly where collaborating with key competitors is concerned—for instance, formation of the tower company as a joint venture between Airtel, Vodafone and Idea—becomes a difficult one for any organization because invariably there will be strong resistance to it at the ground level and it will take a strong top management to decide on it after due consideration without being swayed by popular negative sentiment. Examples of activities/areas that can be outsourced by each industry are innumerable—Cisco and Apple in the high-tech industry showed how manufacturing could be outsourced by still protecting quality and intellectual property rights (IPRs) by combining strict on-site quality control, protection of a secret formula or ingredient (as in the case of Coca Cola and Pepsi where bottling is invariably franchised, but the key potion is always controlled and manufactured centrally) and strong legal agreements with respect to IPRs in particular. In telecom itself, the list is long with the possible inclusion of other passive elements such as optic fibre networks, submarine cable networks, data centres and even active networks and capacities at some stage.

Clarity on compensation for materials and services procured

One area that organizations should focus on is clarity on the compensation model for suppliers of goods and services to get the best out of them in a fair and transparent manner. This would involve the fundamental principle of getting to a win-win situation for both supplier and recipient without compromising on competitive pricing. This aspect is with respect to all procurements of goods and services including but not limited to outsourced activities. The following experiences at Airtel will illustrate some different and innovative approaches to this.

Airtel experience

Outsourcing IT

I earlier described Airtel's experience with outsourcing the IT function to IBM. A key element of this unique approach was the payment arrangement.

Typically, organizations buy IT equipment and software with an outright payment, followed by annual maintenance charges (AMC) and charges for new versions of software and software updates. The people running IT operations and engaged in future development are either insourced or outsourced or both. With IBM, we agreed to pay them a certain percentage of our revenue over ten years as compensation for the investment made by them in hardware and software and the ongoing expenses incurred for maintaining and running all IT services. This included the timely refresh of hardware and software as per pre-agreed norms as well as additional equipment or software required for business from time to time. As the revenue increased (as it was projected to), the percentage was to decrease, but the absolute amount paid to IBM was to increase, thereby providing a win-win situation for both.

Network deployment

As discussed earlier, we decided to entrust all aspects of telecom network operations and services to our equipment vendors.

An important feature of our arrangement with our major equipment vendors—Motorola, Ericsson, Alcatel and Nokia—that we entered into sometime in 2005 was the construct with respect to compensation for the network equipment they were to supply to us.

Typically, in the telecom industry, the equipment is sold as bill of quantities or as boxes, which comprise individual prices for thousands of components, big and small, for each base station to be installed on a tower or for an MSC. We felt that there was an inherent disconnect and conflict of interest in this approach as the vendors tried to sell more and more equipment while the operator wanted maximum coverage and capacity with the least amount of equipment. The other issue was that as per industry practice, only 60 to 70 per cent of capacity created was actually utilized at peak at any point of time, thus leaving 30 to 40 per cent of the investment in capex lying idle perpetually. For a relatively small company like ours, which was growing at 100 per cent per year, such an investment meant a whopping $300–400 million at any point of time.

To overcome the problems mentioned above and to ensure we could expand our network to keep pace with fast-growing demand at the least investment, we asked our vendors to quote on the basis of dollar per unit of capacity created by network equipment supplied by them.

Such capacity was measured in terms of Erlangs and thus the payment was sought to be made for total Erlangs created irrespective of the amount of physical equipment supplied. This popularly came to be known as the 'dollar per Erlang' model in the telecom industry. Based on the likely volume of Erlangs to be ordered, vendors were to quote a dollar per Erlang rate with detailed specifications and SLAs. This move to do away with the box price and go to end-product price was met with stiff resistance by the vendors and within the company initially. The reason was that no one had done this before. Our logic for this move was simple. We argued that if one was to buy a car with given specifications such as the size, weight, engine power, torque, transmission and other features, the discussion would be on the overall price of the car and not on the price of each individual component, for example, the engine, carburettor, tyres, windows, etc. Telecom was the same.

The end product we were buying was capacity, which in our industry was measured as 'Erlangs'. We saw no logic or justification in paying for individual components under a bill of quantities. Our view finally prevailed. For this, we first agreed on a base rate per Erlang, specifying:

1. The total anticipated Erlangs to be purchased in the contract period; and
2. The density of deployment of such Erlangs, that is, the average Erlangs per tower that were envisaged.

The construct was designed to self-adjust the contracted rate depending on deviations from the base Erlangs envisaged and the average Erlangs per site anticipated for the contracted period. The contract provided that in case the volume, that is, total Erlangs purchased in the period, exceeded the base volume, the rate per Erlang would reduce, and conversely, the rate would increase if the actual volume remained below the base volume. Similarly, if the actual density, that is, average Erlangs per tower, was higher than the base density agreed, the rate would reduce and vice versa. Clear formulae were agreed upon for the above adjustments to avoid any need for protracted negotiations. This resulted in a win-win situation for us as well as the vendor in a fair, transparent and logical manner. If we were able to increase volumes above the base level and/or put more capacity per site, we clearly got the benefit of a lower price per Erlang. The vendors too gained because their incremental costs for additional volumes due to economies of scale, and for deploying more capacity on an individual site were relatively small.

On the other hand, if we could not order base volumes or meet the base density, it was only fair that we paid a higher price per Erlang, which compensated the vendor for higher cost per unit due to lower volumes and deployment of more equipment and service costs per Erlang per site.

The other integral element of the arrangement was that Bharti was to pay for Erlangs actually used (at peak) at the end of each quarter and not at the time of installation. To prevent reckless ordering by Airtel, there was an inbuilt mechanism of an end date, say, one year from the date of installation of capacity (long stop date), by when payment would be made for the Erlangs installed irrespective of actual utilization.

The price quoted was to be inclusive of all network planning, installations, customs duties, transportation and warehousing charges and so on, that is, for the actual installed and working network with customary warranty periods and SLAs.

The result was an alignment of interests between vendor and buyer. Both now wanted to have the maximum Erlangs from minimum equipment with better planning. It saved the operator the running expenses on capex, rent, electricity and manpower that came with extra towers, while the vendor gained with full payment (since it was now linked to capacity and not quantity), with least quantity supplied.

Further, the buyer was encouraged to maximize the order in the contracted period so as to avail of the volume discount that was inbuilt in the contract.

The buyer was also encouraged to plan better in conjunction with the vendor so as to maximize capacity at

installed sites to get maximum discounts on higher density
due to higher average Erlangs per site.

Even though the buyer was to initially pay for the
capacity actually utilized, it could not afford to order
in a casual and reckless manner due to the following
reasons:

1. It had to incur recurring expenditure on passive
   infrastructure, that is, site rentals and energy charges
   on towers installed; and
2. Ultimately, it had to pay for the capex on the site
   ordered on the long stop date, irrespective of actual
   utilization.

An illustration of this model is given below.

The dollar per Erlang and Erlang per site models

Assumptions

Period of contract: 1 April 2005 to 31 March 2007

Base assumptions

Total likely volume: 5,00,000 Erlangs
Total Erlangs per site: 50

Rate: $ per Erlang based on
above base assumptions: $800

Illustrative adjustment mechanism for dollar per Erlang model

		Item	Measure	Measure		
A	Base Agreed	Volume	Erlang	500K		
		Density	Erlang per site	50		
		Rate	$ per Erlang	800		
B	**VOLUME**			Base		
	Actual volume	400	450	500	600	650
	% by which lower/higher than base	-20%	-10%		+20%	+30%
	Variation in rate @ 50% of variation in volume	+10%	+5%		-10%	-15%
	Resultant Difference in rate ($ per Erlang)	+80	+40	800	-80	-120
C	**DENSITY** i.e., Erlang per site			Base Erlang per site		
	Actual volume	45	47.5	50	55	60
	% by which lower/higher than base	-10%	-5%		+10%	+20%
	Variation in rate @ 50% of variation in volume	+5%	+2.5%		-5%	-10%
	Resultant Difference in rate ($ per Erlang)	+40	+20	800 (Base rate)	-40	-80
D	ILLUSTRATIVE PRICE DETERMINATION	Case A	Case B	Base case	Case C	Case D
	Volume (Erlangs)	400	450	500 Erlangs	600	650
	Adjustment in price as per B above: I	+80	+40		-80	-120
	Density (Erlangs per site)	47.5	55	50 Erlangs per site	45	55
	Adjustment in price as per C above: II	+20	-40		+40	-40
	Resultant rate per $ Base rate + I + II	900	800	800	760	640

Note : The underlying principle is that in case of shortfall, the base rate is to increase, and vice versa.

As mentioned earlier, this methodology of pricing the capex purchase of an active network was a unique and groundbreaking solution from Airtel. Despite telecom being an old industry, this methodology, which provided a win-win solution for both buyer and seller, was not thought of by any other operator. The concept of dollar per Erlang became attributed to Airtel globally and has often been referred to in the industry as Airtel's dollar per Erlang model.

Charges for network operations and maintenance

This comprised two parts:

1. Maintenance of the active network equipment at a site, that is, preventive maintenance, fault repair, reconfiguration, etc: The charges for all these activities were fixed at a certain rate per month per site with suitable premia for difficult sites/low-density sites, for example, upcountry sites and discounts for city sites with greater density.

2. Annual maintenance charges (AMC): These comprised replacement of parts, maintenance of spares, software updates and version changes, etc. The charges were a percentage of actual capex incurred based on total deployment of Erlangs and were payable on an annual basis post the warranty period.

Passive infrastructure

A major challenge with respect to passive infrastructure outsourcing was to find a sustainable pricing model that would ensure the following:

1. The price charged by the tower company was such that when an operator analysed the self-build versus lease decision, it had no choice but to go for leasing towers from tower companies because of the clear cost benefit. This was aimed at 'disarming' the operator with respect to its organizational capabilities of putting up towers so that for all their tower requirements they would have to go to the tower companies as over time they would have no organizational capability or resources left to do so internally.

2. On an ongoing basis, have a win-win situation for a tower company and its customers (that is the operators) with respect to sharing the benefits arising out of sharing the site.

3. Effective competition with other tower companies not on the basis of price undercutting but on the basis of first mover advantage in having:

   (i) More existing sites in the geography, which would reduce the time to market for an operator; and

   (ii) Lower price vis-à-vis the competition because of the pricing model itself, which has inbuilt discounts for each additional tenancy.

The above objectives were met by adopting a pricing model with the following salient features:

1. Single-tenant rental would be such that it made the operation cash positive but did not fully cover long-term depreciation, for example, on steel towers with a life of twenty-five years or more. For an operator, it was a clear advantage to lease the tower instead of

building it not just because it saved capex but also because leasing entailed a lower overall cost.

2. Successive discounts were built in for all tenants when an additional tenant came on the same tower. This is illustrated in the table below.

Type of tower	Rate per tenant per month (Rs)	Total rent collected (Rs)
Single tenant	30,000	30,000
Two tenants	24,000	48,000
Three tenants	22,000	66,000
Four tenants	20,000	80,000

Similarly, energy charges reduced per tenant with additional tenancies, due to more efficient utilization of diesel generator capacity.

The most important feature was that the existing tenant did not even have to apply for a discount but received it automatically upon a new tenant coming on the tower.

The discount structure wherein each successive tenancy resulted in an additional discount for all tenants posed a significant entry barrier for competitors. This was on account of the fact that if a tower company had a tower with at least one tenant, every operator wanting to set up their network site in the vicinity of that tower had no option but to prefer that tower company. This was due to the fact that a tower company that did not have a tower near the existing tower could not put up a new tower and still charge the lower tariff applicable to a second tenant (which the tower company with an existing tenant would have charged) even from the first tenant. That would be a big loss proposition for that tower company since even with first tenant rates it would not have recovered the full cost as explained above. Further, reduced rates would have made a new tower unviable.

3. Every time an operator added more equipment to an existing tower, he was to pay only an incremental 'loading charge', which was a fraction of the full rent. In an industry where technology changes very quickly, this has been of immense help to operators who have deployed new technologies at existing sites. This has also ensured stickiness as it is virtually impossible for an operator to shift a fully loaded site to another site.

As already mentioned, the unique and innovative approaches adopted in the above-mentioned arrangements, namely, IT outsourcing, outsourcing of network operations and maintenance, separation of passive infrastructure towers into a joint venture with competitors, and the manner of pricing equipment purchases led to all these becoming the subjects of various case studies at Harvard Business School and being taught in MBA and AMP classes. Some of them are also part of the curriculum at the Indian School of Business.

3

Organizational DNA

We often speak of the DNA of individuals, families, groups, communities, religions, tribes and even nations.

Before I give some examples of contexts in which this term is commonly used, let me share how this complex subject has been simply and brilliantly explained by Zoe Gamble on sciencemadesimple.co.uk:

'DNA stands for deoxyribonucleic acid. It's the genetic code that determines all the characteristics of a living thing. Basically, your DNA is what makes you, you! You got your DNA from your parents, we call it "hereditary material" (information that is passed on to the next generation). Nobody else in the world will have DNA the same as you, unless you have an identical twin.'

We often hear that a person's DNA is such that it would never permit them to cheat others or go back on their word. Conversely, we are cautioned that it is in the DNA of certain people to cheat and lie and thus we should not trust them. Similarly, the DNA of some communities is linked to their being hardworking and enterprising, such as the Sikhs. The DNA of others is credited with making them naturally good with numbers, for example, baniyas, while others have the DNA of being mild and sophisticated but still enterprising, such as the Parsi community. Similarly, certain religions like Hinduism are said to have a DNA that makes them tolerant and peace-loving, while some others are referred to as having a DNA that makes them generally more rigid and aggressive. Again, some nations with democratic beliefs such as the USA and India are said to have the trait of being tolerant and transparent in their DNA while some others are said to have a DNA of being authoritarian and secretive.

As a company is a non-living 'person', one could question the relevance of DNA for such an entity. The fact is that since an organization lives beyond the people managing it and particularly in professionally managed companies where there is normally no blood connection between predecessors and successors, it becomes imperative for an organization to have a soul or DNA of its own. This DNA encourages its employees, managers and various stakeholders to behave, think and act on the basis of a basic ideology, the absence of which could lead to arbitrariness and cause mayhem.

Like human beings, good as well as not-so-good organizations come to be known for their 'DNA'. For instance, a good company such as Hindustan Lever is known for its DNA of ensuring that its people grow within the company with the support of training and rotation, with the result that most of the positions are filled internally. On the other hand, there are companies where it is reputed that people are treated as contract labourers, without respect or development plans. The relationship between employees and the organization is transactional and people are known to leave at the first available opportunity to escape from the 'trap' they find themselves in.

Similarly, there are companies such as Disney which are known to have a DNA whereby they look out for minute details that may be causing dissatisfaction to the customer and removing them or training their staff to go beyond prescribed processes to help and delight their customers. For every Disney there are ten examples of companies whose DNA makes its staff look at customers as counterparties for individual transactions, thus making them overlook emotional connects and long-term relationships.

Another great example of the DNA of an organization is the ethical practices and corporate governance that they adopt. In India, companies or groups such as Bharti and the Tatas are known for very high standards in this regard. Needless to say, there will be innumerable companies in India whose DNA would be just the opposite.

To me, one of the most important jobs for the senior leadership and board members of any company is to recognize and register the DNA or basic beliefs of the company and to ensure that irrespective of changes in business, strategy, management, regulation and laws, this 'soul' is preserved and improved. This is indeed a laborious task requiring sustained and serious effort. Some specific actions that can help in achieving this are given below.

Managers and leaders should reiterate, remind and explain the organization's DNA at every possible occasion within the organization.

Explaining the organization's DNA must become the most important part of the induction programme for all new employees, directors, vendors and even advisers.

An organization must follow strict governance policies—internally by way of code of conduct and externally (such as with vendors) by way of contractual obligations (like a no-bribery-or-favours policy).

The organization's DNA must be emphasized in human resources manuals and vision and mission statements.

There should be demonstrable appreciation for employees who exemplify an organization's DNA, and demonstrable reprimands and consequences for employees who do not adhere to it. For instance, many companies like Bharti follow a zero tolerance policy regarding corruption or nepotism/favouritism by an employee, irrespective of his or her capabilities, performance or past contribution to the company. Such actions reiterate the DNA of the organization to all concerned.

An example of how a company's DNA is reflected in its actions can be found in Bharti's formation of Indus Towers. Indus Towers was established in 2008 under an initiative taken by Bharti to pool telecom infrastructure, namely, towers built by Bharti and its two arch rivals, Vodafone and Idea, through an equal partnership joint venture. This initiative was proof of a deep-rooted DNA at Bharti which believed that 'while you can compete fiercely at the front end, there is no reason why you cannot collaborate at the back end and agree to coexist with mutual respect'. This is diametrically opposite to the DNA of most companies, which believe in blocking or even eliminating opposition wherever possible.

I would strongly urge all managements and boards to work diligently to create and nurture organizational DNA. Once that is done, senior leaders and mentors need to constantly communicate this DNA to the rank and file so that it truly becomes the DNA of everyone in the organization.

4

Organizational Structure

Once an organization determines what its DNA or culture should be and has decided on its business model and business delivery model, the next step would be to clearly lay out its organizational structure (OS). The OS is the framework, much like the human body, wherein different parts are assigned specific tasks, but in harmony with other parts. A good OS will ensure the smooth and efficient working of an organization. On the other hand, a flawed OS with lack of clarity on specific roles and responsibilities and reporting structure could play havoc with the organization, leading to internal politics, lack of engagement and constant finger-pointing for failures.

To develop a good OS, the following must be done (each of these have been discussed in detail in Part II):

1. Determine the levels of hierarchy, that is, the number of levels between the lowest-level employee and the chief executive officer (CEO). While it is important to have various levels in a large organization to ensure

decentralization of authority, responsibility and accountability, as also to ensure the proper handling of a large number of people, it is equally believed that the more the levels between a CEO and the lowest employee, the greater the chances of an organization losing alignment and the people below feeling alienated.

Traditionally, large companies typically had twelve to fifteen levels between the CEO and the base level, but now most companies prefer to have no more than six to eight levels of hierarchy. To some extent, this is also due to an overall reduction in the number of employees today on a like-to-like basis versus earlier.

2. Define the responsibilities and authority of each position by laying out a delegation of authority (DoA) for each position. The DoA provides job descriptions of various positions, clearly defining roles, responsibilities and authority. The more the responsibility and authority, the greater will be the level of DoA for that position and vice versa. DoAs are typically suggested by the human resources department and recommended to the board or audit committee by the CEO. A good DoA will ensure a fine balance between robust internal controls and ease of conducting day-to-day business.

3. Base responsibilities and authority on time-tested principles of segregation of duties to ensure there are no conflicts of interest and that internal controls are meticulously laid down.

As an example of a good segregation of duties, the person responsible for placing a purchase order must never be the one with the authority to release payment to the vendor against such purchase order. The reason being that as a process, payment must only be released after an independent check on actual receipt of goods and/or services ordered as well as quality. Giving the same person the responsibility for both placing an order and ensuring that all checks have been duly conducted before release of payment could compromise independence and result in poor internal controls.

4. Lay out the level of seniority required at each level based on the business and delivery models. The qualifications, experience and special skills needed for a position shall depend on its level of seniority.

5. Also lay out the number of people required at each level by way of a periodic exercise to take into account the volume of business achieved and planned in the next year or few years.

6. Define the multiple roles that can be performed by one person for a given duration, depending on the size of business achieved. These roles should not be in conflict with one another as per the principles of segregation of duties. Such multitasking may be required due to several reasons. For instance, the need could arise if a person occupying a position abruptly leaves and a replacement is not immediately forthcoming. Some companies may also test such multitasking temporarily to see if two positions can be combined into one to achieve better efficiencies.

7. The basic OS must be planned for at least two to three years, taking into account the medium-term business plan (MTBP) of the organization. Frequent changes to the OS can create confusion and chaos within the company with significant wastage of time and organizational energy to explain the changes and the rationale behind them. Of course, the number of

people required at each level may have to be reworked to meet each year's annual operating plan (AOP), but this should be done within the defined OS. Conversely, not changing the OS can also be detrimental as an OS must keep pace with the dynamic environment of an organization, which may warrant modifications to the OS to be able to deliver the desired results in keeping with an altered business or delivery model or technological changes or a combination of these factors.

A common mistake observed over the years is the tendency to change the OS based on favourite individuals. To my mind, a successful human resources function must fit the right persons into the OS and not the other way around. Of course, as mentioned earlier, a capable individual can be called upon to perform multiple roles but only those that have been identified as appropriate for multitasking as per the principles of segregation of duties.

I have always believed that an organization need not take pride in stating that it employs many thousands of people. Instead, it should be proud to state that it achieves a high level of revenue by employing a few but highly satisfied and motivated individuals. This can only be achieved through a desired level of automation and outsourcing wherever the principles of outsourcing are satisfied. Revenue per on-roll employee is a good key performance indicator (KPI) to follow. A good OS will serve as the platform to achieve this important KPI. While there are no generic benchmarks available for this important KPI, a desired level would depend on the type of business, levels of outsourcing, level of technology and IT investments made behind various processes and the activities involved.

5

Medium-Term Business Plan and Funding Requirements

All responsible organizations, governments, individuals and families do some future planning to assess resource requirements in light of their plans and aspirations. While some may do it informally, others may do the same in varying degrees of detail and as a formal process.

In most companies, such a plan that covers more than one year would be referred to as a 'business plan'. Depending upon the duration covered, plans are short term (say, up to two years), medium term (say, up to three to five years) or long term (over five years).

A plan or projection for the coming year is generally called an AOP or a 'budget', as most governments (including India) call them.

Many companies take enormous pride in claiming that they have a very long-term business plan—in some cases covering the next thirty to fifty years.

With due respect, in my opinion, while it is good to have a long-term vision, it is only appropriate to have at best a medium-term plan covering at most the next five years. Anything more in today's era of rapidly evolving technology and the introduction of artificial intelligence (AI) would make many activities and even products redundant.

The fundamental purposes of an MTBP are the following:

1. To assess the finances required so that the same can be planned well in advance.
2. To lay out an OS that would by and large remain valid for this duration.
3. To lay down a basic technology design/platform that is capable of being scaled up to the levels envisaged in the MTBP without a complete revamp.

The quality of this MTBP would depend not on the length or depth of detail but on the extent of deliberations amongst the top management and external experts when required, to gaze into the future so as to attain a good balance between being a dreamer and a realist. The MTBP must accordingly reflect the agreed business model and take into account the business delivery model and resources available, thereby setting targets and projections based on logic and practicality rather than on wishful thinking or wild ambitions. It may be advisable to take the help of external experts whenever deemed appropriate to get an independent view on the MTBP, taking into account projected market and other relevant factors—either in terms of resources required and available internally or other information available externally—for example, likely competitive developments or technological changes anticipated. Such factors could have a major impact on determining the level of investment required for technological changes or market development or human resource requirements.

It is also important that this MTBP is prepared on a rolling five-year basis, that is, at the beginning of each year to encompass any major developments that may not have been anticipated in the previous version but that could have a major impact going forward.

6

Means of Financing

As I mentioned before, a major reason for developing an MTBP is to assess the level of financing required over, say, the next three to five years.

While it would be neither possible nor desirable to arrange for the entire capital requirement on day one, a fair assessment of the capital requirement at different stages of the business plan is imperative to ensure appropriate resource planning and to raise capital in a timely manner—both equity and debt.

If on paper it looks impractical to raise the funds required as per projections, it would be important to either prune the plan or identify possible sources of capital that would find the plan acceptable.

I always feel that it is more prudent and practical to have a business plan that is achievable, since at the time of financing, the actual performance for the latest period will always be compared to the last business plan. If projections are achieved or preferably exceeded, a revised plan with higher projections of revenue and profits, even if it has greater capital requirements, will always be more acceptable. Accordingly, it is desirable to have a rolling five-year business plan and to arrange funding requirements there against for at least the next one to two years.

The most important aspect when planning funding is to look at the level of debt planned by the company (leverage). A high leverage can be a disaster, particularly early on in a project's life as in the absence of established profitability, one could easily fall into a debt trap. In the project phase, leverage in the form of debt as a percentage of equity, and after the project phase, in the form of net debt/earnings before interest, tax, depreciation and amortization (EBITDA) are the most accepted measurements.

The levels would differ from industry to industry primarily depending on the capex spend required. However, a prudent level is generally a net debt to EBITDA level of below three times. The logical rule being that the higher the ratio of capex as a percentage of EBITDA, the lower the net debt to EBITDA multiple and vice versa. Liquidity is of the greatest importance and the day a company finds it difficult to pay the interest and/or principal repayment (debt servicing), irrespective of the soundness of its underlying business, it will get into trouble.

On the other hand, it is equally important to have a reasonable level of debt since the required return on equity is always much higher than debt (especially for a tax-paying company as interest on debt is tax deductible) and thus by implication, return on equity in the absence of debt will be much lower.

Let me explain with a few examples for a company with the same profitability (before interest) but with different levels of debt and equity for the same capital deployed in business.

A. Assumptions

		Case I	Case II	Case III
1.	Profit before interest	100	100	100
2.	Capital employed			
	Debt (a)	100	200	300
	Equity (b)	400	300	200
	Total capital employed (a+b)	500	500	500
3.	Rate of interest on debt	10%	10%	10%
4.	Effective rate of income tax	20%	20%	20%

B. Resultant return on equity

	Case I	Case II	Case III
Profit before interest	100	100	100
Less: interest on debt	10	20	30
Profit before tax	90	80	70
Less: tax @ 20%	18	16	14
Profit after tax	72	64	56
Equity	400	300	200
Return on equity that is net profit/equity	18%	21.33%	28%

As is clear from the above illustration, the percentage of return on equity in a profitable company increases with higher debt or leverage.

One practice that I found useful in the early stages of Bharti's business and which I would recommend to all businesses in the early stages is to first focus on getting a commitment for equity (even if it is subject to requisite debt-raising) rather than vice versa, that is, first getting debt tied up and then looking for equity. The likelihood of convincing an early-stage equity investor without debt being in place is significantly better than vice versa.

While I have highlighted the significance of planning for means of financing in the early stages of a company's formation, the importance of this for running projects or companies with established track records must not be underestimated. The advantage for a running company is that it is easier to assess the possibility of raising the requisite finances—both equity and debt—and accordingly adjust the MTBP as per the likely availability of finances.

7

The Management Information System and Key Performance Indicators and Their Measurements

'What gets measured gets managed.'

—*Peter F. Drucker*

Periodic reporting, that is, a management information system (MIS) based on an agreed upon standard format, is the backbone of good governance. The reason is that the quality and effectiveness of governance in any organization is directly correlated to the quality and depth of performance-related information available. If the information itself is either incomplete or unreliable, the analysis of data is likely to be faulty. Any decisions taken on the basis of such an analysis (or no decision or corrective step taken due to incomplete or inaccurate information) would most likely be detrimental to the interests of the organization. This would be similar to a doctor prescribing treatment on the basis of the wrong test results. I recommend that an MIS should be based on and cover the following:

1. Reliable data from the IT system without human interference. For this, the IT systems and enterprise resource planning software need to be robust with very well-defined processes and internal controls whereby no person can alter the results or MIS reports generated by the system.
2. The incorporation of all important KPIs. What those important KPIs could be are discussed separately below.
3. Inclusion of financial as well as operational information. The typical financial and operational information is discussed separately below.
4. Fully audited accounts every quarter which should tally with reported results in all respects.
5. The same data at different places/reports is the same, that is, from same source.
6. A clear mailing list for relevant reports on a need-based basis, avoiding the tendency to mark to all.

The key to a good MIS is the finalization of KPIs to be tracked and analysed. KPIs determine the focus areas for monitoring the progress of a company.

KPIs

KPIs would differ for assessing the overall performance of the company and individual functions such as finance, human resources, technical functions, sales and marketing, etc. Typically, for each assessment, one would select four to six relevant KPIs, assign a score (say, against 100 as the maximum) for each KPI and assign weightages for each KPI depending on the importance of that KPI. These have been discussed in more detail in Part II, chapter one, 'Human resources'.

Below is an example.

Illustration A: KPIs to Assess a Company as a Whole

	KPI	Score	Weightage	Wt. Score
1.	Return on capital employed	90	30%	27.00
2.	Revenue market shares	95	30%	28.50
3.	% of revenue from new revenue lines	110	20%	22.00
4.	Customer satisfaction score	105	10%	10.50
5.	Employee satisfaction score	102	10%	10.20
		Overall		98.20

Illustration B: KPIs to Assess the Finance Function

	KPI	Score	Weightage	Overall
1.	Overall company score	98.2 (as per Illustration A)	40	39.28
2.	Timely tax compliance	95	10	9.50
3.	Timely financial reporting	100	10	10.00

	KPI	Score	Weightage	Overall
4.	Quality and correctness of reporting	120	20	24.00
5.	Leverage targets	105	20	21.00
		Overall score		103.78

Typically, the overall weighted average score would be used to determine what the performance-linked incentive (PLI) should be, and thus KPIs assume great importance for people working in an organization.

Businesses and organizations have KPIs relevant to their needs. Some of the KPIs that would be common to most, if not all businesses, are as under:

Financial performance

1. Reported for the period, say for the month or quarter
2. Year-to-date figures
3. Performance as compared to the corresponding period the previous year
4. Performance in relation to the AOP or budget
5. Quarterly trends of, say, the last five quarters

Some common indicators:

P&L-related

1. Segment-wise gross revenue
2. Net revenue (akin to gross profit)
3. Opex, broken up into three or four broad heads
4. EBITDA
5. Earnings before interest and tax

6. Profit before tax
7. Profit after tax
8. Capex
9. Operating free cash flow (EBITDA—capex)
10. Free cash flow (interest + tax)
11. Net debt (total debt as reduced by cash and bank balance and equivalent investments, for example, in mutual funds, fixed deposits or government bonds, which can be encashed at short notice)

Balance sheet and others

1. Net worth
2. Net debt/EBITDA
3. Return on capital employed, that is, total of debt and shareholders' equity including reserves
4. Return on equity, that is, paid-up capital (including share premium) and reserves
5. Debt-servicing ratio (EBITDA for the year/interest payable and principal repayable in the next twelve months).

Operational performance

These would differ for each business but should broadly cover the following aspects:

1. Units sold, for example, number of cars for an automobile company and number of minutes and data (GBs) sold for a telecom company
2. Price recovered per unit
3. Employee productivity, that is, revenue per employee
4. Total count and cost per employee

5. Number of customers and revenue per customer (for service companies)
6. Broad details regarding fixed assets, for example:
   a) Number of towers for a tower company
   b) Number of BTSs for a telecom operator.

It is important to include all KPIs that are linked to performance analysis of key personnel in the MIS. This helps ensure corrective action is taken by the concerned person if the relevant indicators are adverse.

As you would have noted, in the illustrative list of financial KPIs, the term 'EBITDA' figures repeatedly. There is no doubt that EBITDA is an important indicator of operating profitability and is used to assess levels of leverage as well as to ascertain whether the company's ability to service debt (interest and repayments) is comfortable. However, unfortunately for most companies, this has inadvertently become the sole matrix for judging operating financial performance. Surprisingly, not just the operating teams and CEOs (whose PLI is invariably tied to it), but even the board, audit committees and savvy investors of many companies tend to track this indicator as the sole barometer of performance.

I believe that companies need to move away from this obsession with EBITDA since it ignores interest and depreciation. In industries such as telecom, which are capital intensive and where, accordingly, interest, depreciation and amortization constitute a major component of overall cost, exclusion of these while judging a company's performance not only gives a faulty picture of performance but also gives rise to bad behaviour in terms of decisions relating to insourcing or outsourcing of services involving heavy capex.

If the operating team is judged and rewarded on the basis of EBITDA, they will insist that all capex-related activities must be undertaken by the company internally and never outsourced. The reason for this is that the total cost of any activity that involves capex comprises the following elements, which are explained below with respect to, say, towers:

1. Opex, for example, rent paid to landlords, operational and maintenance expenditure on equipment on the tower (such as AMC), manpower expenses, energy charges directly incurred (such as electricity and diesel), other overheads such as administrative costs
2. Interest on capex
3. Depreciation on capex.

As the term EBITDA—earnings before interest, depreciation, tax and amortization—implies, out of the above, only opex is reduced when calculating EBITDA while interest and depreciation are accounted below EBITDA (popularly known as below the line) to arrive at the net profit.

Accordingly, in the case of self-incurred capex, EBITDA would be higher as compared to outsourcing where all three elements, that is, opex, depreciation and interest, are charged to the company as 'operating expenses'.

Let me explain this with an illustration:

A. Assumptions

		Case A: Self-incurred Capex		Case B: Outsourced
1.	Revenue	1500		1500
2.	Capex on towers	750		—
3.	Operating expense other than on towers	300		300
4.	Total cost Opex on towers Interest on capex @ 10% Depreciation on capex @ 10%	150 75 75	300	300*

* Assumed to be the same as self-owned as the profits to outsourced partner would come from sharing of tower with other operator.

B. Resultant EBITDA and Free Cash Flow

	Case A		Case B	
Revenue	1500		1500	
Operating expense other than on Towers	300		300	
Opex on Towers	150	450	300	600
EBITDA		1050		900
Less: Interest	75		—	
Depreciation	75	150	—	—
Profit before tax		900		900
Capex		750		—
Free cash flow (EBITDA – capex – interest)		225		900

As is clear, even when the total cost of the tower is significantly lower in the case of outsourcing as compared to insourcing and profit before tax and operating free cash flow is much higher in the case of outsourcing, EBITDA is lower in the case of outsourcing due to interest and depreciation being below the line in the case of insourcing.

As discussed in chapter two, 'Business Delivery Model', the decision relating to insourcing or outsourcing needs to be taken based on the three principles of better domain knowledge, better economies of scale and ability to attract better human capital. Fixation on EBITDA moves an organization away from this important decision-making process.

I strongly recommend that the financial performance of any organization and the segments comprising the business thereof must be judged on the basis of return on capital employed. This represents earnings before interest and tax divided by total capital employed by the company, that is, equity, debt as well as current liabilities (in other words, the equity and liabilities side of the balance sheet).

By looking at the return on capital employed, the performances of all companies, irrespective of their capital structure, that is, levels of equity, debt and current liabilities, will become comparable. The fundamental principle behind the return on capital employed approach is that capital employed, irrespective of its nature thereof, is not free.

EBITDA, on the other hand, should only be used to ascertain overall leverage and debt servicing levels. Here, irrespective of impact on EBITDA because of insourcing or outsourcing decisions, the results would be comparable. The reason being that in the case of insourcing of capex, while EBITDA would be high, so too would be its debt (due to high capex) and corresponding debt servicing. On the other hand, in the case of outsourcing of capex, EBITDA would be low but so too would be the debt (due to low capex) and corresponding debt servicing.

One must remember that the ultimate aim of any business should be to give a high return on the capital employed, which would result in a high return on equity for the shareholders.

To a large extent, with the introduction of new accounting standard IND AS 116 relating to lease accounting, this flaw has been plugged. Under this standard, all leases have to now be treated as finance lease whereby the net present value of all lease payments over the contract period needs to be capitalized and thus treated at par with 'self-owned assets' on which interest and depreciation is applied in the same manner as it would apply on 'self-owned assets'. Thus, by and large the EBITDA under the new standard would be at par irrespective of whether an asset is owned or is taken on long-term lease. However, since the method of capitalization in terms of assumption of percentage of 'deemed ownership' is somewhat subjective, the principle of analysis discussed above remains valid.

8

Transparent and Reliable Reporting and Accountability

Transparency and reliability are the two most important attributes that determine the reputation of an individual, a group, a community, a corporation or even a country. Those considered transparent and thereby trustworthy or reliable carry high credibility and vice versa. Credibility gives a major edge in dealings with the external world. For corporations, this element of credibility is of vital importance as it deals with investors, the financial world, vendors and service providers, government and government agencies and even its own employees. Companies that are perceived as being transparent are perceived as having high standards of corporate governance.

For a long time, amongst Indian companies, the Tatas were perceived as being the most transparent, with a general belief that this group had 'nothing to hide'. Unfortunately, in recent times, in the aftermath of the 2G scandal and related enquiries, this reputation has taken some beating.

Later, one company emerged in the IT world—Infosys— which had a stellar reputation in terms of its transparent and reliable reporting to investors, with detailed quarterly reports, investor meets and regular press meets on its state of affairs.

From day one at Bharti, we were clear that if we wished to grow and had ambitions of rapid expansion, we would need to not only follow in the footsteps of these two respected groups, but perhaps even overtake them in this aspect. Accordingly, we, from a very early stage, treated transparent and reliable reporting as a religion. However, the deeper purpose behind transparent reporting to the external world was more internal. We realized that transparent and reliable external reporting automatically ensured the same internally. I can safely say that in the majority of companies—both listed and unlisted—the quality of internal reports is poor and thus unreliable. Our logic was simple. If you want to control large operations in diverse geographies and listed companies, the only way to solve problems at an early stage is to produce high quality reports internally, without worrying about whether the results being shown are good, bad or ugly. Our quarterly reports to investors for our listed companies—Bharti Airtel and Bharti Infratel and recently for Africa as a separate listed company—have become benchmarks globally, not only because they contain financial information that is fully audited every quarter but also because they contain all the relevant operational information that would allow an analyst to assess the state of affairs and project the future. Based on our experience, I am listing below some golden rules that we diligently follow and which I would strongly recommend to all corporations to embrace. I can safely say that this remains my personal favourite obsession.

It is important to ensure that a full financial audit is conducted every quarter.

Further, a quarterly report should be produced, giving all relevant financial and operational information with periodic comparisons and trends over the last five quarters. Items to be included should be based on what a good research analyst would need to know to get a good sense of business prospects. For instance, the report must include financial information such as profit and loss (P&L), the balance sheet, segment-wise performance, key financial ratios such as the EBITDA margin, net debt to EBITDA ratio, the return on capital employed, the return on equity and year-on-year and quarter-on-quarter comparisons. It should also include operational information, for example, for a telecom service, it should give information on total revenue-earning customers, total voice and data traffic and traffic per customer, average revenue per user, number of employees and revenue per employee, network-related details such as number of sites, etc. These reports for Bharti Airtel, Bharti Infratel and Airtel Africa are available on our websites, www.airtel.in, www.bharti-infratel.in and https://airtel.africa respectively, and I would encourage readers to take a look at them to get a better understanding of transparent reporting.

A good report strikes the right balance between relevant information and excessive information. To this end, condense only to the extent that relevance is not lost.

Avoid the tendency to not share information due to it being 'competitive information'. This must be seriously debated since the majority of information typically included in reports does not give any edge to the competition. I feel that withholding information on account of it being of a 'competitive' nature must be an absolute exception and should be permitted only in compelling cases.

The quarterly report is primarily for the use of management even in a listed company. The golden rule is that whatever is measured and reported is also attended to. If some information looks bad, I can say with experience that the manager responsible will invariably ensure that the underlying issue is resolved as soon as possible.

Clearly fix accountability for accuracy and performance for each report and each KPI. There must be an owner for good as well as bad performance.

While everyone agrees that transparency is important, it is well known that the quality of reporting and transparency in most companies in India is not up to the mark, to say the least. In recent times, the number of companies where suppression of critical information (for example, loans taken by a company and given to sister concerns) has been detected has increased dramatically. This is perhaps due to the introduction of the Insolvency and Bankruptcy Code (IBC) whereby defaults in payments of dues are coming to light, leading to forensic audits, which have revealed some shocking facts that were concealed by the management for years from the auditors, audit committees, board and hence the shareholders. The question is, what encourages an entity to be non-transparent? It is generally believed that the pressure of showing good performance quarter after quarter in line with market expectations, the pressure of maintaining and increasing share price and the pressure of PLIs, amongst other factors, are some of the key reasons why some managements resort to the malpractice of hiding or distorting facts. This leads to the other relevant and important question, namely, what needs to be done to promote a culture of being transparent and truthful while reporting both internally and externally? Based on my years of experience, I can say that this is an extremely difficult task because at every step one is urged to part with less rather than more information. I have personally faced situations where my insistence on having quarterly audits was met with stiff resistance, even from some of my board members who felt that such an 'unprecedented' step would put pressure on our finance department and would hamper 'flexibility'. With solid backing from Sunil, we went ahead with performing quarterly audits and producing quarterly reports, which even today are cited as best practices globally. I can say with certainty that a culture of transparency can only be introduced and nurtured by the top management. As part of succession planning at top levels, one of the most important criteria for me would be whether the candidate shares this belief in and passion for transparency.

9

Decision-Making
Based on Analytics

In the previous chapter, I spoke at length about the importance of transparent and reliable reporting, both internally and externally.

However, the purpose of such reports is not merely to gain a good image. The main purpose is that based on reliable data, proper analytical studies are made to determine areas of strength as well as areas that either need improvement or need to be revamped altogether. While the actual analytics and the process would differ from company to company, one thing that is common to all good companies with a proven track record of efficiency is that they use those analytics to make relevant decisions and do not rely on the 'gut feeling' of the promoter or the CEO alone.

In this chapter I discuss the role of analytics in decision-making as well as some pointers on how to best approach decision-making.

Analysis and input for decision-making

The most important step is to analyse the reported data, and based on this analysis, draw up a list of issues categorized as, say:

1. Showing steady progress/results
2. Poor performance
3. Volatile performance with lack of control
4. Some good results, which look too good to be true.

The quality of this analysis and the clarity with which issues are summed up is the most important tool for sound and productive governance.

Analysis must also lead to the framing of questions for decisions to be taken to ensure corrective action.

Decision-making

Issues that require decision-making should be bifurcated into the following categories:

(a) Where no change of agreed strategy or overall approach is required.
(b) Where a change may be required either in strategy or in tactics.

In the case of (a), the decision-making is simpler as it need only be action-specific, within the agreed strategy and approach.

However, in the case of (b), the decision-making approach is complex because it would require revisiting the agreed strategy/approach. This may accordingly require revisiting the business model or delivery model itself as discussed in chapters one and two of Part I.

The suggested rules for conducting meetings leading to specific decisions are discussed under 'Rules of Meetings' in chapter five, Part III.

10

Governance Philosophy

We are all aware that the quality of countries, companies as well as individuals (like children in a family) depends on the quality of 'governance'. In fact, the word 'government' in the context of a country makes this clear since a government is supposed to govern the affairs of a country in all respects—economic, social, law and order, security and external affairs, to name a few. It is also to be noted that different 'governors' or 'managers' or 'governments' will have different styles of governance. Some are very hands-on with consequent concentrated and centralized authorities, while others govern by delegating authority and power. Typically, in terms of countries, heads of government with a dictatorial and authoritarian bent of mind would adopt the former style while leaders with a democratic bent of mind are likely to adopt the latter. It is also noted that for both types there are different shades and scales, to the extent that sometimes the leaders of a democratic nation tend to lean towards the former category. History has shown us that both ways of governing can produce great results over time. Singapore is a good example of this. During his tenure, authority over virtually all matters remained firmly with Prime Minister Lee Kuan Yew, but the success he garnered for his country is legendary. For the exemplary results he produced for Singapore, he is often respectfully referred to as a role model despite being called 'a benevolent dictator' by some.

In my experience, in order to have lasting results, the most important principle of governance is to 'govern by exception'. This term refers to the philosophy of focusing on issues where the results are outside normal parameters—either on the negative or positive side. To illustrate this, let us take the example of a pathology report, say a blood report or a kidney function test. Typically, if the result for a parameter falls outside what is considered the normal range, it is highlighted. This enables the treating doctor to glance through the report but focus on the highlighted results for prompt corrective treatment. The same applies to a company. The manager reviewing a report must quickly be able to focus on issues that are not within typical ranges. If negative, prompt corrective action must be taken. However, if such an exception is a positive one, the manager must analyse the root cause for the positive result so that the contributing actions, strategies or tactics can be replicated elsewhere for similar results.

This principle must apply at every level of the organization and the list of exceptions must keep getting trimmed as governance moves to higher levels.

Accordingly, while the top level of an organization must be aware of all relevant and material facts and developments by way of a robust MIS, the focus should be on a few exceptions, both positive and negative.

For example, normally, the acceptable level of performance would be benchmarked to a projection in the AOP for specific items. This could be revenue, EBITDA margin, return on capital employed, return on equity, net debt/ EBITDA, revenue market share, etc. Depending on the nature of the business, the level as per the AOP is extended by a certain percentage, say 5 per cent on either side, to form an acceptable or normal level. For instance, if the EBITDA margin as per the AOP is 40 per cent, then 38 per cent to 42 per cent could be designated as an acceptable band or level. Any performance indicator that falls outside this band would be an exception and should thus be noted and actioned upon.

Governance by exception promotes empowerment and accountability at all levels. This is on account of the fact that people take pride in knowing that if they perform well, they will not be constantly questioned and will be given the freedom and power to discharge their duties. With empowerment automatically comes accountability. Many organizations suffer because managers insist on doing in-depth 'reviews' of every aspect. In the process, they often miss out on the exceptions that need their attention and decision-making. In addition, at the top level, it frees the mind to look at strategic interventions that could have a material impact based on facts and analysis of material exceptions.

A suggested governance process is given in chapter four of Part III.

11

Knowledge Management and Internal Controls

> 'Knowledge has to be improved, challenged and increased constantly, or it vanishes.'
>
> —Peter F. Drucker

Every organization gains knowledge during every day of its existence as it experiences different situations, problems and solutions encompassing a large variety of issues covering finance, customer experience and complaints, processes set up for various activities, fraud, reporting and so on. Invariably, in a large organization, different experiences and issues will arise in different parts—disciplines as well as geographies and business segments.

In my experience, a successful organization is one that systematically manages and uses the knowledge that it generates each day. The basic purpose of knowledge management is to fulfil a central theme, namely, that to help ensure that an organization does not repeatedly face the same problems or issues, a systemic and sustainable solution to each problem must be provided and then applied across the organization.

The steps to achieve this end are as under:

1. Establish a system of information whereby issues that have an adverse impact or any act that improves the efficiency of an activity are reported and captured at a central point. The best point for such collation is the internal assurance group, which many organizations call the internal audit group. I will further discuss this group later in this chapter when I talk about internal controls.

2. Set up a focused specialist team within the internal assurance group, which, in conjunction with subject matter experts on the issue involved, conducts in-depth root-cause analyses to ascertain the causes behind issues that arise. These causes can typically be categorized as:

   • People-related
   • Process-related
   • Technology-related
   • OS-related

The quality of the root-cause analysis will determine the quality and effectiveness of the ensuing solution.

3. Once the root-cause analysis has been completed, the next and most important step is to find a solution that addresses the causes. This could involve a

multidisciplinary team to cover all aspects, particularly human resources, IT, the specific discipline to which the issue primarily relates and in most cases, finance. External experts should also be used whenever required to ensure quality.

4. The solution so decided should then be documented along with any required changes to the delegation of authority and segregation of duties—IT software and systems, operational processes or human resources processes as the case may be.

5. The next step would be to communicate and implement those changes across the organization. Normally, the internal assurance group at each level of the organization would be the custodian for such a change with direct responsibility and authority lying with the concerned head at that level/segment.

I have stated earlier that the internal assurance group is the best focal point for knowledge management. There is an important reason behind this. You will have likely noted that every organization of some size has an internal audit department. Generally, the purpose of this department is to thoroughly check mainly financial and related records to ensure that matters/compliances that might escape the attention of statutory auditors are duly screened to ensure their accuracy.

I feel that this is a bit of a myopic view and undermines the true importance of this function. I believe that the best utilization of this skill set is to ensure that there exist robust and effective internal controls over all important financial as well as non-financial activities so that these are always performed in accordance with regulations. A good organization has to necessarily depend on controls that it imposes internally (and hence the name internal controls) to ensure the existence of safeguards against fraud or misuse of authority.

The knowledge management discussed above is a part of strengthening those controls and hence the natural connection between knowledge management and the internal control group.

Since the job of this group is to assure that suitable controls exist and that checks have been carried out to ensure that those controls work, the ideal title for this group would be 'internal assurance group', which would make it responsible for internal controls as well as for checking compliance.

To illustrate how knowledge management would work, let me take you through an issue that we experienced at different group companies over time.

Issue

A vendor was supposedly paid for an outstanding invoice for which provision was made in the books, but the cheque was encashed by an unauthorized entity which opened a bank account in the name of said vendor.

Root-cause analysis

It was seen that despite there being a proper delegation of authority and segregation of duties requiring two unconnected persons to clear such payment, an unauthorized payment had been cleared. The reason was that one of the persons responsible for clearing the payment was very casual with his password, enabling an unauthorized person to clear it by using his password.

This was therefore both a people issue and a process and technology issue.

Process

The flaw also lay in the process for recording vendor details. It should have been ensured that when registering a vendor, their bank details were obtained. The process should also have provided for either payment to be made directly to the vendor's account via a direct remittance system called RTGS (real-time gross settlement), or if a cheque was issued, to ensure that it automatically included the name of the vendor's bank and the account number, without human intervention. The absence of these enabled an unscrupulous element, in connivance with our employee, to deposit the cheque in a bank account bearing the name of the vendor by giving the wrong know your customer (KYC) documents to that bank. There was also a flaw in the process of managing passwords.

Technology

A major cause for this lapse was that we had not implemented the feature in our enterprise resource planning system that enabled direct authorization to a bank for payment to the account of a vendor as given in his master record or printing of a cheque by the accounting software itself giving such bank account details.

Also, the use of biometrics instead of normal passwords should have been introduced to avoid misuse of passwords.

As another example, in one case, it was observed that the OS was faulty in that the segregation of duties was not proper. Two persons from the supply chain management department itself were authorized to clear payments. The correct structure to authorize payments would have been authorization by two persons belonging to two different departments—one from supply chain management and the other from another function, say finance.

12

Dealing with Complexity through Simplicity

'Any intelligent fool can make things bigger and more complex . . . It takes a touch of genius—and a lot of courage to move in the opposite direction.'

—*Albert Einstein*

'That has been one of my mantras—focus and simplicity. Simple can be harder than complex. You have to work hard to get your thinking clean to make it simple. But it is worth it in the end because once you get there, you can move mountains.'

—*Steve Jobs*

One of the biggest problems in the corporate world—to my mind—is the obsession with making issues and matters complex. Unfortunately, this problem multiplies as the number of 'experts' in each discipline increases.

This happens in all disciplines including the basic common sense ones such as finance, marketing, sales and distribution and human resources—leave alone the more technical functions or IT, which have elements that a person outside that discipline would not understand.

Let me give you a few examples. In finance, the finance guys like to talk about interest rates with even non-finance guys in terms of 'basis points' rather than a simple rate of interest in percentage terms. In marketing, the most fashionable term is 'customer life cycle', which, by the way, has nothing to do with the demise of a customer, but somehow it is believed that every customer has a limited shelf life with a company.

The list is endless. And when it comes to technical disciplines such as networks, IT or law, a person who is not from that discipline can often feel like he is being spoken to in a foreign language.

My belief is that such behaviour, where every discussion or presentation is filled with jargon and complex diagrams, arises out of insecurity where a professional fears that if everyone understands what he is saying, he will lose his status as an 'expert'.

At Bharti, we have always had a golden rule whereby an 'expert' is defined as one who can explain the most complex issue in such simple terms that it can be understood by the person at the lowest level in the organization.

It is my belief that by sounding complex and 'specialized', one can keep others in awe, but if you want results which in turn will need team effort, you better make sure that the team understands the issue and the solution that it is working on.

To me, this is an important part of the DNA of an organization and the responsibility for this lies at the top, to inculcate simplicity as a way of life. In doing so, 'experts' will accuse you of 'over-simplifying' complexities and therefore courting disaster. Nonetheless, I feel it is better to oversimplify than to overcomplicate.

13

Going Public or Remaining Private

'The good parts about being a public company are increased discipline, increased execution and increased transparency to make sure that you are really building a company for a hundred years.'

—Dan Rosensweig

There is a popular saying in India, *'jungle mein mor nacha kisne dekha'*, which means that no one sees a peacock dancing in the jungle. In other words, for talent to be appreciated and followed, one does have to step out and be seen by the world, outside the confines and comforts of one's habitation.

Imagine the fate of great leaders such as Mahatma Gandhi or Nelson Mandela or great sportsmen such as Roger Federer, Sachin Tendulkar, Pelé, Tiger Woods, Virat Kohli, M.S. Dhoni or Michael Schumacher if they had decided to remain in the comfort of their club teams or small groups rather than advance to more public platforms.

For a company, to my mind, this is the equivalent of being private or unlisted versus being public or listed.

Those who remain 'private' as persons or companies fail to grow beyond a point while those who decide to go on a public platform can grow in skills and stature beyond imagination. A fundamental reason for this is that being 'private' confines one's experiences to a limited radius, like a frog in a well, and consequently limits the ability to compete and excel or see one's flaws. On the other hand, a public exposure ensures comparison and competition with others and the opportunity to meet persons who can help one improve and excel.

In the corporate world, there are examples of many companies that remained private and did very well. However, of these, only a few have survived or survived without being acquired by listed companies.

I accordingly firmly believe that an organization should decide at an early stage whether it would like to be publicly listed at an appropriate time or remain private.

I also believe that this decision will inherently reflect the DNA of the organization since the desire to be listed invariably prepares the organization to be transparent, lay great emphasis on accurate reporting and be accountable for its performance. On the other hand, an intent to remain private would reflect a somewhat closed and secretive mindset, which could result in vital facts being brushed under the carpet in the garb of not sharing 'competitive information'.

My personal view is that for anyone venturing into a business, the aim from day one should be to scale it up to a level where it can be listed. This would obviously involve public scrutiny and curb the mindset of absolute control, irrespective of equity holding. To my mind, listing is good not only for all shareholders and other stakeholders but also for the company in terms of its ability to raise finances, get ratings and attract good partners and talent within the company.

This, however, remains a contentious issue for most owners, in India at least, with a large percentage preferring to remain below the radar to have the so-called freedom to act without having to seek approvals or give explanations to public shareholders.

I strongly recommend that if one is prepared to follow high standards of corporate governance and transparency, listing is the best way forward for a company.

14

Unique Selling Propositions

'If you don't distinguish yourself from the world, you will just be the crowd.'

—*Rebecca Mark*

We live in a competitive world where in most cases, competitors operate with the same or similar technologies, tools and offerings. The success of an organization in such an environment lies in its ability to continuously create 'unique selling propositions' (USPs).

Contrary to popular belief, a USP need not be limited to technical aspects; it could be on any other parameter—customer service, loyalty programmes, tariffs, etc. As an example, Emirates created a USP by giving free transportation to and from the airport for business and first-class passengers. Creating USPs is a culture that every organization must instil. Since a USP may not remain unique for long, as competition may copy it, it is imperative to develop a 'USP factory' where USPs are conceived, planned and tested continuously and then released at periodic intervals. It is noteworthy that in every business and every product or service offering, there is always scope for introducing USPs. In another example from the aviation industry, Indigo created a USP by designing a ramp to replace the stairs typically used when an aircraft does not get a berth at an aerobridge. Customers can virtually slide down this zig-zag ramp. This not only ensures the quick turnaround of the plane but also provides relief to people with knee problems or those on wheelchairs. You will find examples of USPs in every walk of life and in every industry. Examples include the introduction of tubeless tyres in the tyre industry, the introduction of a 'meter' displaying the level of discharge in batteries in the energy storage industry, the introduction of single-use sachets for shampoo, face wash, etc., in the cosmetic industry, and so on.

It is not important to have several USPs at any given point in time. What is important is to have one or two important USPs, and the moment one or more cease to be unique, introduce new ones that have been created in the USP factory and are ready to launch.

This approach has been very successfully taken by Intel in terms of their microprocessors. The world always wondered how, within days of their competition matching their last launched product, they were able to introduce a new advanced version. The answer is that they had perfected the USP factory and that as a matter of strategy, they would have two or more new versions at any point but would release them one at a time depending on whichever one was ahead of the competition. I feel this is a very important rule to follow for every company seeking leadership.

It is clear that companies which are known to introduce USPs regularly are perceived as leaders and command a premium, for example, Samsung in the television segment, while those that are constantly chasing to match the features offered by their competitors without introducing USPs themselves are certain to be perceived as laggards and will lose market share. Most of the Japanese television manufacturers have been falling in this category of laggards in the last five to six years.

15

Fixing It When It Ain't Broke

'If it ain't broke, don't fix it is the slogan of the complacent, the arrogant *or the scared. It's an excuse for inaction, a call to non-arms.'*

—*Colin Powell*

Thomas Bertram Lance, the director of the Office of Management and Budget in President Jimmy Carter's 1977 US administration, made an important, famous and practical statement: 'If it ain't broke, don't fix it.' While he said this in the context of government functioning, a lot of corporates also tend to follow this religiously.

On the other hand, there is a very famous military saying: 'The more you sweat in peace, the less you bleed in war.' This saying, attributed to General Norman Schwarzkopf of the US Army, who fought in the Vietnam War, the Gulf War and the invasion of Grenada, has become a mantra in militaries across the globe.

These two famous sayings are diametrically opposite to each other, and contradictory. Wise as they are, they often create confusion amongst individuals and corporates in terms of action, behaviour and mindset.

I, for one, am a great believer in the latter saying, that is, 'The more you sweat in peace, the less you bleed in war'. My reason is simple. The improvements, transformations and innovations that one can plan, implement and experiment with when things are going well (peace time) can never be achieved when there is crisis and chaos. In a crisis, one can only engage in firefighting as one does not have the luxury to experiment with new thoughts.

My belief was reinforced when I attended an advanced management programme at Harvard Business School. A senior and respected professor there—Professor William E. Fruhan—introduced a novel concept, which he called 'the power of D'. 'D' stood for 'dissatisfaction'. His theory was that for an organization to stay on top, it must invent a self-programme to create internal dissatisfaction even when everything was functioning smoothly and with great results. His logic was the same—that in times of peace and prosperity, if one followed the saying 'If it ain't broke, don't fix it', then one would turn the organization into a lazy and rusty outfit, with the result that when things actually broke down (which they will at some point), it would not be ready or have the resources to deal with the situation.

I accordingly would strongly advocate that every company create a group that will continuously analyse performance on different parameters—particularly during the heady days of success. It is inevitable that even when a business is going through a successful phase, there will be some aspects on which it is underperforming and some where even if its performance is good, there is scope for improvement. Such improvements will invariably involve a change of processes or delivery model or both. Most companies will not attempt to change such issues, since they 'ain't broke'. However, I feel that the smart and progressive ones are those who in times of success and prosperity have the guts to challenge themselves and change the approach and/or processes for better performance on specific matters, even if such changes do result in a temporary slowdown or minor disruptions. The resources and margin of error available for bringing in disruptive changes when a business is doing well are much better than when things actually break down. The trick, of course, is to not go overboard and become trigger happy, bringing about change for the sake of change. The organization must be ready to sweat it out, thinking through and planning the changes so as to get maximum benefits with minimum disruptions.

PART II

General Rules for Some Specific Disciplines

Different disciplines, such as human resources, finance, IT, legal, etc., are like individual artists in an orchestra. The success of the concert depends on how well each artist performs individually as well as as a team. This section deals with some common issues faced by each discipline.

1

Human Resources

'Train people well enough so they can leave. Treat them well enough so they don't have to.'

—*Sir Richard Branson*

Of all the disciplines, I believe that human resources or HR is the most difficult, complex and important one to handle across geographies and across industries.

In the previous section I discussed the need for an organization to have a DNA. An organization's DNA is manifested through its employees, and hence the handling of employees becomes critical.

Almost every organization claims that 'our people are our biggest strength'. This is indeed true, but what is politically incorrect to say but equally true is the fact that 'our people if not handled well can be our biggest weakness'. This can be particularly true for an organization with a large number of employees. The reasons being indiscipline, rivalries and egos, the tendency of some to cheat and defraud, non-adherence to the code of conduct, dissatisfaction and disengagement due to a plethora of reasons from compensation to lack of authority to lack of recognition, etc.

Accordingly, the biggest effort today across industries globally is to reduce the workforce by either automating tasks or outsourcing activities. Today, when there is a raging debate about loss of jobs due to automation and AI at all levels and industries and the social ill effects thereof, it is politically incorrect to support automation with a view to reducing the number of employees.

I have to admit that I have always been a big and open advocate of automation at every level, from the shop floor of a factory, to the accounts department, to call centres, security, maintenance services and any other activity that one can think of that has repetitive actions, with the aim of reducing manpower.

The reasons are clear. Machines produce a better quality output as they meticulously follow laid-out processes. They do not demand restrictions on working hours or overtime, they do not demand promotions or increments, they do not sulk because some other machine received better treatment. As a result—and particularly in an environment like India where double-digit increments in compensation every year are a norm—despite a big capex on a machine and a normally higher cost initially vis-à-vis the human counterparts doing that job, in the long term, machines are more cost-effective, directly and indirectly.

Having said that, it is impossible to replace the entire workforce with machines. In this chapter, I discuss some important aspects of HR, which, as per my experience, are critical to making the people in an organization a formidable and powerful tool in the pursuit of its goals.

HR organizational structure

The first and most important task is to have a clearly designed OS that defines how the organization is manned to execute the business model (with agreed delivery model) in an efficient manner with the least amount of friction amongst people at the same or different levels in an organization.

The key factors to keep in mind when developing an HR structure are as under:

1. It should be a lean structure with no more than five or six layers from the very top of the organization to the very bottom. Anything more needs to be carefully scrutinized as it will invariably reveal duplicity of roles, underutilization of managers or avoidable tasks.
2. It should be based on clarity of roles, responsibilities and authority at each level.
3. It should follow the principles of internal controls such as segregation of duties to ensure that the roles assigned do not result in conflicts of interest.
4. The roles that can be assigned to a person as additional responsibilities, that is, multitasking, for short or long periods, should be identified. These would need to be selected based on the principle of no conflict of interest and in conformity with internal controls.

Selection of a person for a specific role as per structure

A fundamental mistake that many organizations make is to mould an organization's structure based on individuals. The result invariably is a faulty structure with overdependence on select individuals whereby organizational growth suffers.

It is imperative that the exercise of designing an OS is done on a 'blindfold' basis whereby existing employees are kept out of sight and it is assumed that all recruitments are to be afresh. Having arrived at the right structure, the existing employees should then be fitted into appropriate positions and not vice versa.

The above exercise will ensure that the organization is robust, with the right person in each role.

Career and succession planning

In my experience, a common shortcoming in HR is lack of career and succession planning. If one desires a healthy growth environment and engagement from employees, it is important that career as well as succession planning is done for at least every senior person (ideally for everyone in the organization) as an annual exercise. The career planning exercise must clearly spell out, with the knowledge and concurrence of the employee, the career progression planned for that employee over the next three to five years (subject, of course, to agreed performance levels being achieved). This exercise will help keep the individual engaged and will also avoid impractical expectations on the part of the concerned individual. There is no point in promoting someone if they keep falling short of expectations. It is better to part ways with an employee whose career progression aspirations in terms of levels and/or time frame are at significant variance with those of the organization. I have seen innumerable cases where a person has been disappointed with their growth even when HR and his or her boss felt that they were on a 'fast track'. A common issue that needs to be discussed early on is choice of discipline/direction that the individual would like to pursue vis-à-vis what the organization would like him or her to do. For instance, it is common to see smart managers in the finance or marketing disciplines having aspirations to move into general management roles (for example, CEO/head of a circle in the telecom industry), while the organization would like them to rise in the said stream itself, for example, growing the finance manager to be financial controller or CFO of a vertical and later CFO of the company/group. There is a real danger of losing bright minds if this conversation is not had with them and alignment achieved regularly.

Needless to say, HR must have a system of tracking the actual progress of the individual versus planned progress. If it is considered necessary to deviate from the agreed path, it is critical to have an open and honest dialogue with the person concerned explaining the reasons for the deviation—whether it is unsatisfactory performance or a change in the growth plans of the organization.

It is my belief that as part of the DNA of an organization, we must let a person know if they have hit the glass ceiling within the organization. We owe it to our people to let them pursue their careers (even if it is elsewhere) in line with their own assessments of their abilities and provide them with the time to look out for opportunities and help them out with references, if required, provided there are no code of conduct issues. I have often heard of organizations keeping an individual on as he or she is currently needed in the role that they are performing, even at times by extending false hope. A good organization must have it deeply ingrained in its DNA that as an employer, it is part of its duty to develop its people and help them grow and not destroy their careers.

At Bharti, we take enormous pride in the fact that our former colleagues are in leadership positions in different organizations across industries and geographies. The practices as above, if followed sincerely, will result in them being our 'ambassadors' for life.

Conversely, those who leave because of false promises having been made to them become bitter critics for life. At Bharti, as in any organization, we too have a few in the latter category, which is unfortunate and are clearly cases of bad handling. The redeeming factor is that the Bharti ambassadors for life far outdo the bitter critics. A good organization must aim to minimize, if not eliminate, people leaving the organization because they are disgruntled or feel cheated in any way.

Simultaneously, HR must have a process of succession planning for each such individual for whom it does career planning. It is inevitable that even with the best of career planning, some people will want to leave because of better job offers or for other reasons. This is particularly true for organizations that are successful and leaders in their field. Such organizations do become great hunting grounds for talent required by others in the same industry or even in other industries.

Proper succession planning will ensure that there is never a void due to certain individuals leaving suddenly. This is generally so in organizations that aim for at least 80 per cent of vacancies to be filled by internal candidates. Good companies such as Hindustan Lever have followed this practice diligently over decades, and after some initial failures, Bharti is now trying to follow this as a rule. This results in the person next in line being given proper and structured training to step into a higher role at short notice.

A big dilemma facing HR in this respect is that the designated/identified successor may not be fully ready to take on the new role. Accordingly, the temptation is to recruit the successor with the best fit for the job from outside the organization. Top management must lay down a strict rule that even if the internal candidate scores say 70 per cent to 75 per cent of the external candidate's assessed score, the internal candidate should be preferred over the external candidate. The reason is simple. The effort required to ensure that an external hire fits into the organizational culture and ways of working and absorbs the relevant institutional knowledge is invariably significantly more than the effort required to plug the shortcomings of the internal promotee. I am sure that like me, the experience of most senior managers across functions and industries would lead them to favour internal promotions.

Training and retraining

A necessary outcome of a structured approach towards career and succession planning is programmes for regular training of individuals to prepare them for their next role. Part of this programme would be to impart training directly for that role and part to train an individual to understand the impact of other roles and disciplines on the role being planned for them. Besides equipping the person to be better prepared as a successor, it also promotes team spirit, with each individual (particularly at senior levels) appreciating the significance of various roles and the difficulties faced by people in other functions.

At Bharti, we pursue a structured policy of imparting trainings such as 'finance for non-finance executives', 'IT for non-IT', 'marketing for non-marketing', etc., at regular intervals. The results have been successful, and I strongly recommend that every organization diligently pursue this policy.

Compensation structure

The four components of the compensation structure for an individual in an organization are as under:

1. Fixed component: To be paid each month/at each agreed interval.
2. Variable component: Linked to performance and paid either annually or at agreed intervals.
3. Long-term incentive plan (LTIP): As the name suggests, this is an incentive payable to an employee over a longer period of time than just one year. This incentive is normally given either at the end of a fixed year—say at the end of the third year of employment with the company, or in parts each year, say a third each over three years. This is a very effective tool for the retention of deserving candidates as it gives them a portion of wealth creation by the shareholders and/ or a reward for staying with the company.

    LTIP can either be in the form of cash payments or by way of the option to acquire shares of the company (but not an obligation) at a given price called 'exercise price'. This is popularly known as employees' stock options (ESOPs).

Cash is a simple form of LTIP where a certain sum of cash is assured to the employee at the end of a specified period(s). This is suitable for employees at lower levels who need or prefer the certainty of receipt of reward.

An ESOP, on the other hand, does not assure the employee of gain, though it ensures that he will not lose money if the share price falls. This is because the employee is given an option to acquire a certain number of shares of the company at the exercise price, but he is not obliged to do so. This means that if the share price at the time of acquisition is more than the exercise price, the employee gains. Conversely, if the share price by that time has dipped below the exercise price, the employee is under no obligation to exercise his 'option' and thus under no circumstances would he suffer a loss.

Let me explain the way ESOPs work with an example.

Assumptions

- Total cost of an employee to the company per annum — Rs 1.5 million
- Percentage of total annual cost to be given as LTIP — 50%
- Amount of LTIP — Rs 0.75 million
- Share price at time of grant of option — Rs 100
- Exercise price agreed — Rs 50
- Calculation of number of options:

Amount of LTIP/share price – exercise price $= \dfrac{7,50,000}{(100-50)}$

Number of options granted   = 15,000
- Vesting schedule that is no. of   = 15,000; end of year 3
  options that can be
  exercised at what time
- Maximum period to exercise   = 7 years

Illustration

	Case A (Where share price at time of vesting is above exercise price)	Case B (Where share price at time of vesting is below exercise price)
Share price at issue of grant	100	100
Share price on date of vesting	200	30
Exercise price	50	50
No. of options	15,000	15,000
Gain (+) on exercise	15,000 x (200–50) = 2.25 million	Nil
Loss (–) on exercise	N.A.	Nil*

* The reason for no loss is that the employee would not exercise his option as the share price at INR 30 is below his exercise price at INR 50. In this case, he can wait till the end of the seventh year to exercise, if the share price goes beyond the exercise price.

ESOPs can either be by way of actual shares (mostly used in the case of listed shares) or virtual shares (popularly known as phantom stocks). The word 'phantom' signifies the fact that actual shares are not acquired. Instead, a notional calculation of profit on exercise of option at exercise price vis-à-vis an agreed value per share (which could be either based on market price in case of a listed company or a valuation based on a pre-agreed formula or by external independent valuers) is made and paid in cash by the company to the employee instead of issuing actual shares.

4. Perquisites: These are normally by way of provision of a car for personal use, house rent, insurance charges borne by the company, statutory or voluntary contributions by the employer such as Provident Fund, Employees' State Insurance (ESI), gratuity or even expenses on family holidays.

Each organization, irrespective of industry, will need to balance compensation to its people within the above categories. This balance will depend upon the seniority of an employee. For instance, generally at junior levels, the fixed element will be high with some variable element and only minimal perquisites and no LTIP at all.

On the other hand, for senior employees, where continuity and retention are important, the fixed component is generally smaller with a bigger emphasis on the other three, particularly on LTIP. Whatever be the split in any organization for different levels, one common feature that I strongly recommend is cost to company, or CTC, as it is commonly referred to.

To assess the CTC, each component must be valued in monetary terms and the employee should be told his total CTC so that he appreciates each element. For ESOPs, the value of benefit would normally be the amount of benefit based on share price and exercise price on the date of grant (as illustrated earlier). However, in some companies, the value is calculated based on likely share price on date of vesting versus exercise price. To arrive at the projected share price, methods such as Black-Scholes or its variants are generally used.

One component that rides over and above the four mentioned above is 'convenience' or 'assistance'. This could be in various forms ranging from taking care of all procedures involved in insurance claims to a concierge service for the deposit of documents, bill payments, arranging for family trips, etc. The perceived benefit from these services for an employee is generally far greater than the actual expenditure incurred as the employee gets that invaluable feeling of being cared for by the organization. I would strongly recommend extensive and liberal use of this component.

The concept of CTC makes it easier and more scientific to carry out compensation surveys and to determine relative costs at different positions. It also makes it easier for individuals by providing some flexibility within the four elements, as long as they total up to the agreed CTC of the individual. I recount an incident where a particular individual, for whom socially it was very important to be seen as 'senior' with an expensive car, opted to go for a far more expensive car than recommended for his level by taking a reduction in some other element such as fixed pay and variable pay.

Appraisals, KRAs, increments, promotions and payment of PLI

While it is recommended to have a system whereby feedback is continuously received and provided to employees for early corrective measures, it is a good practice to have an annual appraisal.

For such an appraisal to be productive and effective it is important that there is alignment between the appraiser and the appraised on key result areas (KRAs) agreed along with the methodology for calculating the percentage achieved at year-end vis-à-vis targets.

It is generally agreed that there should not be more than five or six KRAs for each individual. These should be spread over the four elements comprising the balance score card approach, namely, financials, people, customer (internal and external) and processes. The weightage and number of KRAs for each element will vary according to position.

Another strongly recommended general principle is that each KRA and performance against it must be measurable so that a score is worked out as a percentage of a target score of 100. To avoid excessive subjectivity in assessment and thereby avoid nepotism and favouritism, it is recommended that at least 80 per cent of the target score must be based on measures that can be scored objectively, that is, based on facts and results, and only a maximum of 20 per cent should be left to subjective assessment.

In many companies, once appraisals have been done, the categorization of individuals in different categories of performance is done by using the 'bell curve' methodology. The bell curve method of appraisal is a forced ranking system imposed on employees by the management. Through this system, the organization tries to segregate the best, mediocre and worst performers and nurture the best and discard the worst. This segregation is based on a relative comparison of performances in similar activities. The bell curve method assumes that employees can be divided into three groups:

- High performers: Top 10 to 15 per cent
- Average performers: Middle 75 to 80 per cent
- Below average performers: Bottom 10 per cent.

The predefined boundaries normally result in the force fitting of employees, with managers being lenient or strict in the assigning of ratings based on given percentages in each category. This normally results in subjective appraisals, which invariably cause dissatisfaction and heartburn across an organization.

To my mind, a more scientific and hence better method is to rank all individuals on a percentile basis, based on natural appraisal, that is, without artificially adjusting the score upwards or downwards (as in the case of the bell curve approach), with the best performer being at the hundredth percentile and others being at different percentiles according to their individual scores. The segregation into the three categories as discussed above becomes transparent and objective under this method.

Similarly, for the PLI payout, it is necessary that rules are preset. For example, if the target performance score of KRAs for the payout of the 100 per cent target PLI is 100, it could be specified that for a score below 80 per cent, the PLI payout will be zero, while for a score above 125 per cent, it would be capped at 150 per cent of the target PLI. Many companies make the mistake of making the PLI payment a 'cliff' at 80 per cent. Say a minimum 50 per cent of the target PLI is at 80 per cent but 0 per cent is at 79.9 per cent. What should be done is to work it out on a gradient basis. For instance, if the target PLI, that is, 100 per cent PLI, is to be given at a performance score of 100 per cent while the PLI would become zero at

80 per cent of the performance score, it would mean that a fall in performance score by 20 per cent would result in the loss of 100 per cent of the PLI. In such a scenario, instead of the cliff approach as given above, it would be more appropriate to specify that for every percentage point fall in performance, the PLI would reduce by 5 per cent. Accordingly, while at 80 per cent it would be zero, at 81 per cent it could be 5 per cent. This could be pre-fed into a program, thereby eliminating the need for human interaction in the calculation of PLI payouts once KRA results have been fed into the system.

Similarly, on increments, rules could be specified for a percentage increment based on percentiles. For example, a 10 per cent increment for those in the ninety-fifth to hundredth percentile, 7 per cent for those in the eighty-fifth to ninety-fifth percentile and so on. I firmly believe that removing so-called 'human interventions' when dealing with human beings leads to overall higher satisfaction. It must be remembered that most human beings are satisfied with their own compensation and increases but are dissatisfied if they feel they got a worse deal compared to some other individual with the same results as their own. A challenge in setting this rule is standardizing it across various segments, divisions and levels within an organization. This must be ensured since a significantly liberal approach taken by one wing can cause huge dissatisfaction to all others.

Communication

Communicating across the organization has never been easier given the availability of sophisticated audio/visual technology and social media today. Most organizations tend to communicate with their workforce at regular intervals through either physical or virtual 'town halls'.

I have two suggestions to make such communication a powerful tool for engagement and motivation. One, most organizations tend to only share good news and achievements. What truly engages people is when along with the good news, the organization shares problems, bad news, failures and plans to combat those with them. That is when they feel that they 'belong' and trust the senior management.

Two, besides the top boss, that is, the CEO, people also like to communicate with their immediate bosses and managers one level up. They feel more connected with them, especially in large organizations where the top management is too far removed. Some suggestions on this are given in Part III, chapter twelve.

Work–life balance

One of the most debated topics today in the context of HR is work–life balance. In too many organizations, people complain of a lack of this balance, with too much pressure in terms of work hours or timelines.

My experience tells me that while such organizations may look happening and dynamic on the surface, they are actually chaotic and suffer from poor planning practices, invariably displaying the problems of unproductive work and processes. An organization that is perpetually firefighting is bound to burn down sooner or later. Unfortunately, many of these organizations actually take pride in 'overworking' their employees.

I firmly believe that if an organization suffers from this syndrome, it must urgently introspect and recheck its business model, delivery model, organization structure, processes and its culture. If people cannot generally finish their work within normal business hours, either the organization is wasting time in doing unproductive work or it has the wrong processes or wrong people at the top. Of course there will be exceptions for some urgent tasks from time to time, but these must strictly be exceptions and not become rules.

It is common practice, for instance, in most organizations to produce a large number of detailed reports regularly. Most of them are not even read, leave alone analysed. Such reports are a good example of unproductive work. A simple solution would be to stop producing a particular report from time to time. If the absence of the same is not noticed, it should be dumped altogether.

Talking of work–life balance, I am a great believer in the philosophy of my boss and dear friend Sunil Mittal, who invented the 'reverse Monday syndrome'. It is a fact that world over, the largest number of heart attacks and stress-related medical conditions arise on a Monday when people are supposed to return to work after the weekend. What Sunil mandated to everyone in the organization was that they were to ensure that every person in the organization was itching to get back to work on Mondays. If not, he wanted such persons to 'shake their boss by the collar' and let him know what was causing them stress.

I strongly recommend that every organization of every size and across industries and geographies adopt Sunil's mantra with zeal and honesty. If adopted in earnest, I guarantee there will be no work–life pressures because the best and most enjoyable part of life would be work.

Incidentally, some of the most successful CEOs across the world observe strict working hours and have a great life beyond working hours with their families and friends and in fulfilling their hobbies. One person in the Indian context who has been successful across decades and who follows this steadfastly is my friend Aditya Puri, CEO of the most successful private bank in India—HDFC Bank. He actually takes it to an unbelievable level by not taking any calls on his mobile after working hours. He is a great example of living a good life while enjoying work and succeeding at it.

On the flip side, people who are far too interested in 'life' at the cost of 'work' need to be parted with at the earliest. People need to realize that they are responsible for performing serious tasks and that the workplace is not a club.

Encourage entrepreneurs, innovation and out-of-the-box thinking

To me, a great organization is one that encourages a culture where people work and behave like entrepreneurs. This culture encourages people to think out of the box and come up with solutions and processes that are simple and efficient and thus improve productivity. A regimented workforce that has been tutored to follow the rules without thinking can be a great machine but will never be able to contribute to improving ways of working or think of new strategies and tactics that an organization must adopt over time. The best knowledge and wisdom lie within an organization. Good top managements work to take the lid off and encourage people to voice their thoughts and views.

I would also recommend that organizations which do outsource certain tasks and activities as part of their business delivery model must try to turn good employees into entrepreneurs by outsourcing the activity(ies) in which such an employee specializes to him whereby he would cease to be an employee and become an outsourced partner/vendor of the company. Our experience at Bharti is that such partners are successful and productive since they know those tasks well and can bring an 'inside out' view when performing those activities.

At Bharti, we take pride in ensuring a culture of entrepreneurship, which has led to some great results over the years and many innovations. These have been discussed at length elsewhere in this book, particularly in Part I. This wonderful culture of innovation and entrepreneurship that all of us at Bharti are proud of and treat as an inherent part of our DNA received befitting recognition recently when I was awarded the Ernst and Young Entrepreneur of the Year award in 2017 (in the category of Entrepreneur CEO) for forming tower companies. To us, this was an honour given to the entire organization for inculcating the spirit of entrepreneurship at all levels, rather than to an individual. Some specific suggestions on encouraging out-of-the-box thinking and innovation are given in Part III, chapter six.

2

Marketing

'The aim of marketing is to make selling superfluous.'

—*Peter F. Drucker*

'Marketing is too important to be left to the marketing department.'

—*David Packard*

Marketing is an important contributor to the success of any organization. Most of the time, it is used as an extension of sales and distribution, which I feel is wrong. Marketing involves decisions regarding products to be offered, pricing decisions including promotions, and branding and advertising. The fundamental purpose of marketing is to create USPs either by way of products on offer, pricing packages and/or by way of brand and advertising and even packaging. What follows is sales and distribution.

Products

Let me start with one of the most important aspects of marketing—products. Products for a company could either be the products or services or even pricing packages being offered to customers. For example, in the fast-moving consumer goods (FMCG) segment such as toothpaste and other beauty products in India, a new company operating under the brand name Patanjali came up with a new product line based on herbal ingredients, which has seriously challenged global leaders operating in India for decades, such as Hindustan Lever (a subsidiary of Unilever), Colgate, Procter & Gamble and Nestlé. Today, Dant Kanti, the toothpaste brand of Patanjali, gives tough competition to established leader Colgate while Patanjali noodles are effectively challenging Nestlé's Maggi noodles.

Universally, when deciding products, the business model adopted by the organization must be kept in mind. For instance, for a company such as Mercedes Benz, which clearly has a model to cater to the luxury segment of the auto market, it would be a disaster if their marketing department were to come out with a mass-market product in the low price range, where Maruti Suzuki is the undisputed leader in India. Another good example in India is Oberoi Hotels & Resorts, which in my experience offer the best luxury hotels wherever they operate. They decided to also participate in the big upper mid segment of five- and four-star hotels. Initially, they started with the brand Oberoi for that segment as well. For example, in Mumbai their luxury hotel is called The Oberoi but the adjoining bigger hotel, which is a few notches below The Oberoi, was earlier called Oberoi Towers. They subsequently brought such hotels under the brand name Trident, thereby clearly delineating two different products on offer, each with different customer expectations and different price points.

The other aspect of successful marketing vis-à-vis products is of course USP, as pointed out in the case of Patanjali.

I recommend that a good practice for all marketeers would be to have a designated person constantly scan the universe for any USPs in their industry globally. Sometimes, unique propositions come from unlikely smaller companies and are worth replicating. Copying USPs introduced in a market other than your own should not be a matter of shame.

Product innovation need not be confined to the actual product or service offered. It could be in terms of pricing proposition. For instance, in telecom in India, Airtel introduced in the early nineties a concept called 'lifetime validity' whereby prepaid customers could recharge their balance with unlimited validity, leaving them the freedom to decide the time period over which they consumed the balance on their accounts. This was a unique offering since all other companies had limited validity products. The logic was simple. Even if a customer did not make outgoing calls within a limited period, Airtel still earned revenue as although incoming calls were free for the customer, we earned either the interconnect charge from the other operator or the outgoing call charge from another customer on our own network. This 'product' become such a hit and USP of Airtel that long after it was copied by others, the term 'lifetime' came to be associated with Airtel—much like bottled water was called 'Bisleri' in India, irrespective of which brand it was offered under.

Brand and advertising

The second most important (and often wrongly considered to be the main or only) function of marketing is branding and advertising. It is unanimously agreed that advertising is a major tool for creating the brand of a company.

Some universal rules or guiding factors vis-à-vis advertising and brand creation and promotion are outlined below.

Advertising has to gel with the product and the image that it is intended to convey. For instance, for a BMW 7 series or a Bentley it would be bad advertising to focus on mileage per litre, whereas for a Swift or Alto, that would be the most important aspect.

Advertising and therefore brand must always follow the fundamental DNA and ethics culture of an organization. For instance, if your organization believes in non-discrimination based on sex, it must stay away from sexually provocative advertisements. However, for a condom company promoting safe sex, sexually provocative advertising would be fine.

In other words, the brand personality that should be the guiding spirit for all advertising must be carefully built keeping the business model and thus the target audience in mind.

The choice of media or mediums for advertising is again based on some globally accepted principles. For instance, if the product is offered in a limited geography in a country, it may not be worthwhile to advertise on national television, which would be very expensive. For such a company, local alternatives such as regional television or metro channels, and billboards, kiosks and local newspapers may be better options to provide best cost per view.

Advertising must always strive to attain a balance between air cover (such as TV, radio and digital), local outdoor presence (billboards and kiosks) and point of purchase (PoP) presence.

I have seen innumerable cases where companies have launched expensive TV campaigns but have very little outdoor coverage and worse still, very poor PoP advertising. The effect is great brand awareness but poor sales, since lack of PoP presence may make a customer decide to purchase another brand due to great advertising at PoP.

It is also imperative that no advertising campaign is undertaken unless the distribution and thereby supply of the product at PoPs is ensured. There can be nothing more annoying for a customer than to be told that the product he intends to buy (as a result of great advertising) is not available on the shelves. This also harms brand image.

Another aspect that should always be kept in mind is consistency of message across all mediums at a given point of time. Consistent messaging results in more effective reach whereas different advertisements or messages on different mediums at the same time could easily end up confusing customers.

Many companies and marketeers believe in 'sporadic' advertising where they advertise heavily over a short period of time, that is, in a 'burst', and then withdraw for many subsequent months. I firmly believe this is a flawed strategy. Marketing must ensure a certain consistency of advertising throughout the year. In terms of total rating points or TRPs—used for measuring TV viewership—I find it useful for a company to specify the average TRPs per month it intends to achieve, say 750 TRPs per month or 9000 TRPs per year, with a specified maximum of 1000 TRPs and minimum of 500 TRPs in any given month. The reason is simple—an important part of human psychology is 'out of sight, out of mind'. I have often seen that a few months of silence, even after a huge burst of advertising, inevitably leads to the perception that the company has fizzled out or is not doing well.

Ultimately, every company must have an advertising spend that provides the biggest bang for the buck. For many companies catering to the younger population, digital advertising works out to be the most effective.

Finally, it is true that brands are about much more than advertising and the brand equity of a company is determined by the way it works and behaves with its stakeholders, customers, employees, vendors, shareholders and society at large on a day-to-day basis. That is why every employee and intermediate, for example, a retailer, is a brand ambassador of the company. Their daily actions determine the equity of the company.

Pricing and promotions

The third important pillar for marketing is pricing, including promotions. In most companies in many industries, pricing is very complex. The telecom industry has been the best, or say the 'worst', example of this with a multitude of plans—often running into hundreds—with little differentiation and with many 'conditions apply' in fine print. It is my belief that for an average telecom customer it is impossible to decipher the real offering. In the process, they at times end up buying what is not the most suitable plan for them. Many a times I have seen managers pride themselves in making customers pay more than what they should for an ideal plan. To me, there cannot be a worse example of destruction of brand image in the long term. This applies to many industries across geographies.

Some of the golden principles that a good marketing outfit should adopt vis-à-vis a pricing strategy are described below.

The pricing schemes should be simple to understand and there should be a few price propositions to suit different segments of customers.

Price plans, particularly in a mass market product company such as telecom or FMCG goods, should reflect 'more for more' as a concept. In other words, customers who pay more in terms of absolute amount must get more value per unit within a category of offering. For example, if in telecom a customer recharges for a high denomination, he must get better value either in terms of rate per minute or value per MB for data, or more minutes and MBs on a proportionate basis vis-à-vis lower denomination recharges. Most FMCG companies use this principle effectively whereby the per-unit price for a small sachet is much higher than that of a big pack with higher price in absolute terms. Reliance Jio has done a good job in introducing just a few telecom tariff plans, which are simple, applicable across India and are based on the more-for-more principle.

The pricing strategy must follow a robust and honest process to calculate end realization in any offering after accounting for promotions, discounts and freebies. Thereafter, the principle of more for more must be tested.

Pricing should generally follow a disciplined approach vis-à-vis competition whereby the effective price charged by a market leader should be somewhat higher than that charged by the nearest competitor. This is on account of the fact that the leader must command some premium over rivals. Also, keeping a premium will prevent a price war since in the event of a challenger offering the same price as the leader, the challenger will have no option but to reduce prices and create a gap. Such premium percentage should be decided based upon the revenue market share gap—the higher the gap, the more the premium and vice versa. Conversely, where one is a challenger, one must keep pricing on a like-to-like basis at some discount to the leader. If the challenger does not offer a discount, the demand will naturally tilt in favour of the leader and the gap in market share between the challenger and the leader could widen. Again, the percentage of the discount should depend on the gap in terms of revenue market share.

Although it would seem to be an obvious strategy, there are innumerable examples of mispricing whereby leaders end up offering a discount while challengers end up with a premium over the leader. The result in the former case is a 'race to the bottom' since the challenger will invariably have no choice but to lower prices below those offered by a leader. In cases where a challenger keeps a premium vis-à-vis the leader, its revenue market share will keep falling.

For the above, it is important to keep the right balance in terms of centralization and decentralization of pricing decisions. Many companies commit the mistake of over-decentralizing pricing decisions at the ground level, which does not allow for a holistic pricing strategy keeping in mind the overall competition in the overall market—

say all India—and carrying it to individual geographies. Often, the result is that an over-aggressive approach in one market leads to retaliation by competition in other markets where they may be in the opposite position vis-à-vis revenue market share. The result, as I said earlier, is a race to the bottom. Many industries such as telecom have long suffered because of this.

It is important for a responsible marketing head to communicate these principles and rationales to the entire team. If not, invariably in the quest for growth in revenue market share, one will get caught in a whirlpool of profitless growth.

Finally, it is important to avoid frequent pricing changes. Frequent changes lead to confusion—at point of sale and at customer service—poor communication to customers and lack of proper planning. Perhaps the solution to this, especially for industries such as telecom where the introduction of new plans and promotions on a daily and at times hourly basis is the norm, is to severely restrict the number of people in the marketing department. Most of the time, new offerings become the proxy for justifying the existence of a large marketing department.

3

Sales and Distribution

'If 80 per cent of your sales come from 20 per cent of all of your items, just carry those 20 per cent.'

—*Henry Kissinger*

'To build a long-term successful enterprise, when you don't close a sale, open a relationship.'

—*Patricia Fripp*

Sales and distribution as a function has undergone massive changes over time. The transformation of this function—which earlier was associated with 'feet on the street', like warriors on a battlefield (the bigger the army the greater the chances of victory)—to a lean machine armed with instant analytics is due to making sophisticated technology available to salespersons. With the availability of online information on all aspects of sales to the sales force through sophisticated software on tablets as well as to channel partners, there are a few practices that can help make this critical function successful and efficient.

Technological tools

By providing technological tools to salespersons, we can get real-time transfer of data relating to:

1. Actual sales, that is, the total revenue generated at a specific retail point/shop and the revenue split amongst different products or plans on offer to customers;
2. The inventories available for each product at such retail points;
3. Automated data analysis for each retail point, the distributors handling such retail points, as well as for each city, each region, each circle and finally, all India.
   With such automated data analysis available online, the number of managers conducting that analysis will reduce. As a result, the sales organization can be 'delayered' or made 'flat' with better direct contact between sales managers and the workforce.

With this, an organization can significantly increase the scope and potential for individual employees, thereby making them more productive, engaged and satisfied with a better working environment and higher compensation.

Commissions

The commission paid to channel partners, be they distributors, retailers, online merchant partners, etc., has always played an important role in end results vis-à-vis sales.

The right structuring of commissions can be a vital tool to achieve the best results for an organization as well as its channel partners. Some of the rules for this are as under:

1. Incentivize the right behaviour. For instance, if a telecom company wants to sell recharge coupons of higher denominations in absolute terms, it must incentivize the channel partner with a higher percentage of the amount of recharge as commission. Most companies make the mistake of having a uniform percentage for all denominations. The result will invariably be more sales of lower denominations as they have a natural pull for customers (especially in emerging markets). To be able to sell a higher-denomination voucher, while a more-for-more offering to the customer (discussed in chapter two on marketing) is needed, the same more-for-more principle must be applied to channel partners as well by offering a higher percentage as commission on such higher denominations. The combination of the right pull and push incentives will invariably result in the desired outcomes.

2. Like pricing in a competitive environment, the commissions to channel partners need to be scientifically determined based on the market position of a company. Accordingly, if one is a leader, the commission should be a little lower than that offered by the seller with the closest market share and so on. Conversely, as a challenger, the commission percentage needs to be a little higher than that offered by the nearest player in terms of market share above the challenger. If not, the

commission percentage will keep rising in an upward spiral.

Apple is a great example in this regard. With the massive pull they have created, its commission percentage is always the lowest in the market vis-à-vis its competitors.

Internal controls

In most trades (if not all), there are always some unscrupulous elements amongst the channel partners. It is imperative to have strong internal controls to ensure that they are unable to resort to undesirable practices.

Let me give the example of a practice that is prevalent in the telecom world. It is a general practice, especially in emerging markets where the battle for new customers is often intense, to give a much higher percentage as commission on a recharge by a new customer, that is, someone who buys a new SIM, as compared to the commission on a similar recharge by an existing customer. For instance, if the normal commission on a recharge of Rs 500 by an existing customer is 4 per cent, the percentage for a new customer could be as high as 25 per cent or even more. The result often is that the retailer tries to convert a regular customer who comes in for a normal recharge to a new SIM by offering a big discount out of his extra 21 per cent commission. The fact that incoming calls are free and that most phones support dual SIMs encourages the customer to retain one permanent number and keep changing the other for outgoing calls. Over a period of time, it has become a rampant practice amongst some dealers to introduce fake new customers based on copies of documents provided by genuine customers.

In many instances, SIMs have been sold to customers who do not want to undergo the process of KYC separately (even at a premium because of ease to customer).

The reasons for such malpractices are:

1. The channel partner is given a big incentive to produce new customers, which has been treated as a KRA.
2. Poor internal controls since the net commission to channel partners on these new customers, that is, commission paid less activation or one-time fee charged, should not have been allowed to exceed the commission paid on a normal recharge.

The result has been that the telecom industry today suffers badly from 'rotational churn', with churn percentages being as high as 10 per cent or more every month, that is, technically the entire base churning out in a year. The term rotational churn refers to a situation where either a large number of customers join the network but leave soon after availing themselves of the promotional offer, or customers shown as joining are non-existent and have been introduced as new customers by unscrupulous retailers who make higher commissions on such 'acquisitions' as explained above.

Unfortunately, sales and distribution is one discipline where internal control is generally an alien concept.

Accordingly, it becomes the responsibility of top management to inculcate a culture of internal controls and logical KRA-setting for each function.

Technology and data analytics

To facilitate controls and the determination of right result areas and performance indicators, an organization must make an extra effort to support the sales and distribution function by putting technology in the hands of salesmen so that information on sales and inventories becomes available online. As explained earlier, since the information on sales as well as inventory would be available online, the sales team will be able to take corrective action in case of low sales of specific products or at specific points as well as quickly replenish inventory when it falls below desired levels. In the absence of such tools giving such information online, it would take weeks (as it used to earlier) to collate data, analyse it and take corrective action. In addition, emphasis must be laid on data analytics to make the best use of the latest information to decide on a future course of action. For instance, if a particular product or offering sells extraordinarily well, it must be quickly analysed whether the offering is at an overall price that is detrimental to the organization and is killing other good products. If not, other products and offerings should be tested to ascertain whether they offer good value to customers.

Such technology and analytics should become the basis for performance reviews of individuals and for setting KPIs.

Incentivizing the internal sales force

While incentivizing trade partners to achieve desired results is important, it is also important to ensure that incentives to the internal sales force are aligned with such results. Logical as it may sound, there are innumerable instances where KPIs for sales staff are set at variance to KRAs desired, based on which market incentives are designed.

For instance, if in an automobile company, heavy incentives are given to dealers for sale of higher-end models but the sales staff is incentivized based on the total number of cars sold, the desired result of selling more higher-end vehicles will be difficult to achieve as the internal sales staff will not be aligned to that objective and will focus on the sale of low-end models, which sell in larger numbers. In fact, they may end up having a conflict of interest and actually discourage sales of higher-end models on some pretext or the other.

4

Technology and IT

'The first rule of any technology used in a business is that automation applied to an efficient operation will magnify the efficiency. The second is that automation applied to an inefficient operation will magnify the inefficiency.'

—Bill Gates

'Our intuition about the future is linear. But the reality of information technology is exponential, and that makes a profound difference. If I take 30 steps linearly, I get to 30. If I take 30 steps exponentially, I get to a billion.'

—Ray Kurzwell

Technology and IT are ever-changing and have undoubtedly become and will remain the biggest weapons for success and efficiency. Technology and

IT, as discussed earlier, enable the availability of vital information and data analytics online, bring efficiencies in production by replacing human beings in repetitive jobs (for example, on an assembly line), result in better quality by eliminating human errors, lead to better long-term cost efficiencies with asset utilization 24/7 and bring capabilities that average human beings cannot even attempt to have. As an example, before the introduction of accounting software and enterprise resource planning, the best of companies and even banks had their accounts written manually. It used to naturally take months before the final accounts were prepared—particularly in the case of large companies and banks with hundreds or even thousands of branches. Today, with automation, such collation and consolidation takes just a few days. To many young readers this would sound unbelievable as they are used to seeing accounting software such as Tally being used today in even small organizations. But when I was doing my chartered accountancy in the late 1970s, the biggest organizations including the mighty State Bank of India used to prepare their accounts manually. The advent of technology has indeed transformed every industry all over the world. With advancement and improvement in technologies assured over time, without doubt such transformation shall continue. Thus, organizations will have to adopt changing technologies to remain relevant and competitive. However, while adopting a new technology, it is important for every organization to be clear on a few aspects. These are outlined below.

Position vis-à-vis technology

A company must decide where it wants to be in the pecking order vis-à-vis technology and IT innovation. The choices could be as under:

1. A research facility to develop, test and introduce new technologies, for example, Tesla for electric vehicle technology or Google for driverless cars.
2. A clear leader in the adoption or introduction of new technology, for example, AT&T or Korea Telecom for 5G or Uber for driverless cars.
3. An early adopter of new technology but not the leader, for example, major telecom operators in the developed world for 5G, major car manufacturers for electric vehicles, etc.
4. A follower in the introduction of technology post favourable commercial terms and proven functioning of that technology, for example, telecom operators in emerging markets for 4G or 5G.
5. Leading the development of use cases on new technology, for example, application development companies using technologies such as AI (artificial intelligence), AR (augmented reality), VR (virtual reality), social media platforms, IoT (Internet of Things), etc., and service providers like telecom companies that bring those developments to their customers seamlessly.

Let me give a practical example from the Indian telecom industry in this regard.

Ever since the introduction of the private sector in telecom services back in 1995, the industry has been clear that it will fall in category (4), that is, introduce technology only when it has been technically proven for deployment on the large scale required in India and is available at price points that make a good and feasible commercial case given the very low tariffs in India. If an Indian telecom company had tried to become a leader in the adoption of a new technology, or involve itself in research for new technology, it would have been bankrupt many times over as the scale, financials, tariffs and average revenues in India could never have supported such a misadventure.

Understanding technology from a commercial point of view

It is normally believed that understanding technology must be left to 'technical experts'. However, for a company to be successful in the adoption of a technology, it is imperative for top leadership, irrespective of their functional expertise, to understand the commercial aspects of the technology— for example, its total cost per unit at different volumes. If the cost falls drastically as volumes increase due to negligible incremental cost, such a technology would be suitable for deployment in the mass market at a low sale price to achieve high volumes quickly, which is possible in a country like India.

On the other hand, if cost does not reduce much with greater volumes due to high incremental costs, then the technology would have to at best remain as a niche offering at high price points.

This point is nicely demonstrated by the telecom sector in India. Mobile service, where cost per minute or MB falls sharply with increasing volumes (because of fixed spectrum cost, low incremental cost in increasing network traffic generating capacity on an existing site, negligible increase in operating charges for towers), was quickly offered as a mass market product at very low tariffs, which enabled its adoption across the country with unimaginable increase in volumes, resulting in lower costs and higher profits. This was against the then existing belief that mobile service was a niche high-price product while wireline on fixed telecom was a mass market product. A clear understanding of this commercial aspect gave rise to the commercial model of purchase of capacity under the dollar per Erlang model (discussed extensively in chapter two of Part I), which transparently showed end cost at different volume levels, leaving no scope for ambiguity or misinterpretation.

On the other hand, fixed line services, where the overall cost did not reduce much with volume because of the physical layout of the network to doorstep, quickly became a niche offering with high minimum price commitments from the customer.

Once this aspect is clear, the next responsibility would be to make it understood by all so as to bring alignment in approach.

Why technology and IT

Whenever a decision must be made on whether or not to invest in the deployment of technology and IT, an organization must determine what purpose such a deployment would serve.

Does the new deployment make life easier and more efficient for the customer? A great example is online transaction capacities, be it bill payment information, queries (Google), payment transfers and remittances (online banking), purchases and sales (e-commerce), transportation (Uber and in future driverless cars), self-care (in telecom, choosing bill plans, or in the airline industry, self check-in, seat selection and meal preferences) and online tracking by customers (logistics companies such as DHL and other courier services).

Does the technology result in the betterment of employees? This could be in the form of providing information relating to pay details, tax deductions, provident fund contributions, availability of facilities such as healthcare, provisions regarding code of conduct, self-assessment and self-appraisal, queries to management on any issue relating to employment, online skilling and training, etc.

In other words, does the technology make life and work easy for employees and help them improve their productivity, quality and speed of delivery, thereby leading to efficiencies as well as job satisfaction improvement?

Does the technology help shareholders gain a better valuation of their equity holding? Transparency, robustness and timeliness of information on all material facts and developments result in better corporate governance, which in turn enables a company to get higher than industry average multiples for valuation purposes.

Does the technology lead to the betterment of other stakeholders?

These could include:

1. Vendors, by way of information on the status of outstanding invoices, leading to online and timely

payments, information on performance of products and services supplied by them, information on future volume expectations, etc.

2. Distributors and retailers, by way of information on features of products/services sold, changes in tariffs/ prices, analytical information on their performance and earnings, online information on the best-suited product/package for each customer (thereby increasing customer loyalty and repeat sale for seller), etc.

3. Investors in equity and debt by way of information on the performance of the company, both financial and operational (for example, through quarterly reports, webcasts, mass conference calls, etc.) and trend analysis thereof to enable them to make informed decisions. In addition, information relating to material developments such as merger and acquisition activity, dividend distribution, rights issue, buy-back, new lines of activities, etc., can be given to investors on a real-time basis.

4. Government and government agencies by way of information on industry performance, tax contributions and likely future volumes to enable the government to plan for the future.

Does the technology lead to improvement in business performance and efficiencies? This can be by way of:

1. Analytics, enabling quick and correct tactical and strategic interventions besides long- or medium-term planning.

2. Analysing customer preferences and enabling cross-selling and upselling, for example, sale of financial

products such as insurance and mutual funds to regular customers.

3. Savings in costs, both capex and opex, due to increased productivity and speed of implementation, resulting in better profitability, cash flows and stronger balance sheets.

4. Improving the basic culture and DNA of an organization by making it an analytical and fact-based organization rather than one based on perceptions and 'gut feelings'.

Does the technology provide much-needed security for the company? This can be by way of:

1. Ensuring the physical security of the premises with regular scanning for security breaches through CCTV coverage and use of access controls, such as retina scans, fingerprints, passwords, etc.

2. Digital security of company information in terms of data storage/mirroring technologies to ensure disaster recovery and prevent unauthorized access to digital information as well as unauthorized transfer of confidential information.

3. Security of field staff with technological interventions such as sensors to ensure safe working conditions. These are particularly helpful in high-risk industries such as mining, fishing, deep sea explorations, infrastructure creation and maintenance in risky areas like hilly terrains, etc.

4. Cybersecurity by providing impregnable firewalls to all IT systems to repel cyberattacks. This equally applies to governments and government agencies.

Companies must pay serious (and at times seemingly disproportionate) attention to security. Investments in sophisticated and specialized IT systems, sensors, network operating centres, and predictive and current analytics must not be compromised. This is one area where external help from experts, including engagement of firms specializing in ethical hacking, must be welcome.

5

Customer Service

'If you are not taking care of your customer, your competitor will.'

—Bob Hooey

'Your most unhappy customers are your greatest source of learning.'

—Bill Gates

A ll companies profess a deep commitment to customer service and customer care. However, the majority end up paying lip service to this idea and justify poor customer care through reasons such as volumes, lack of trained manpower, non-availability of desired/required IT tools— the list is endless. To separate an organization from this majority and to make customer care a part of organizational DNA, I suggest following a few golden rules.

An organization should strive to eliminate the need for a 'care' service by ensuring that customers are always well taken care of. It is important to realize that no customer ever wants to talk to a company. They do so only when a company's products or services do not perform as expected or they do not understand the products or services offered. Take utility companies such as telecom or electricity, for instance. I do not know of a single customer who wants to get in touch with their service provider unless forced to do so due to disruption or bad quality of service, incorrect or unexplained billing (shocks such as in the case of international roaming in telecom), or to understand complicated and ambiguous plans and features announced by the company.

In the event that a customer does need to contact a company, it is important to ensure that they are able to do so online, that is, via the website (rather than by way of a telephone call), with instant or quick response and resolution. It should only be in exceptional circumstances that a customer should need to speak to a person for the resolution of a query/complaint.

When structuring its approach, an organization should focus on 'more for more', that is, give more attention and resources to bigger customers who are fewer in number but contribute to a large proportion of revenue. A universal or 'democratic' approach to providing the same level of customer service to all customers is impractical. For example, in the airline industry, first- and business-class passengers and frequent flyers will need to be provided with better customer service than other customers.

An organization should invest big and invest early in AI to deal with customers. AI can handle customer queries/

complaints much better than humans by way of access to past data and history of customers and ensuring follow-up on commitments made in terms of timelines to the customer. Use of robots or 'bots' for dealing with customers is fast gaining momentum, with companies such as Google taking the lead.

Needless to say, investment in AI and bots must be accompanied by a commensurate investment in analytics to predict problems that are likely to be faced by a customer. For instance, in telecom, with sophisticated tools and software, predicting the likelihood of a customer leaving the operator based on recent interactions with a call centre or variations in traffic patterns is now quite robust and reliable. Timely actions based on such AI have allowed telecom companies to retain many such dissatisfied customers in the nick of time. With the introduction of the Internet of Things, such predictions will be available to all industries as sensors will be able to predict breakdowns and malfunctions much before they actually happen.

As technology can play a big part in ensuring quality customer care, a company must invest adequately in training and retraining of frontline agents and backroom persons employed in customer service so as to ensure that they stay abreast of the latest technological interventions and processes.

Most companies are misled by so-called customer satisfaction surveys conducted by external agencies which are appointed by the management. It is no wonder then that almost all such surveys show the appointing company to be stronger in key aspects vis-à-vis the competition and perhaps weaker in not-so-important aspects. To kill this conflict of interest, it would be in every company's interest to get a common, industry-wide survey done where the results of other companies are reported on a no-name basis. Thus, a company would get to know its own ranking vis-à-vis common measures without knowing the scores of other companies, which would in turn prevent them from running down opponents.

It is also important to note that perhaps such external customer surveys will lose their utility in times to come given the prevalence of social media, where customers freely and without solicitation post what they feel about a company, its products, prices, services or general aptitude. Good companies must provide a robust platform to encourage customers to post their frank opinions on these aspects. Such unadulterated feedback along with the use of AI and analytical tools will be the best surveys available to management (particularly senior management) to provide timely and appropriate customer care.

Another effective tool is the engagement of outside experts to do 'mystery shopping' as actual customers of the company on each aspect of customer experience in different service/sales areas. The results of such an exercise are more reliable since mystery shopping does not report on the performance of a company vis-à-vis its competitors and is thus more acceptable as the concerned individuals within a company do not feel the need to get defensive.

Finally, to improve customer care, it is imperative that the results of all surveys and reports are communicated regularly and transparently to all concerned—internally as well as externally—and not sporadically or on a selective basis, thereby sharing good news and suppressing bad news. This is akin to the need to have a good quarterly report covering financial and operational aspects in a standard format, irrespective of good or bad results.

In my experience, companies that have the guts to share bad news both internally and externally are the ones who correct shortcomings the quickest as responsibilities for corrective measures are quickly assigned.

6

Audits, Reporting and Business Performance and Analysis

In my experience, most companies fail or perform poorly on account of one or more of the following:

1. Unreliable and inconsistent reports, results and performance indicators
2. Lack of transparency in reports and reporting
3. Non-availability of required information to the right persons and/or at the right time.

The above factors invariably result in lack of alignment amongst team members as they tend to see and perceive different performance levels or get information that is unreliable or untimely.

The following rules, if strictly followed, will help prevent this situation (which, incidentally, we all face in varying degrees, despite our best efforts).

Management information system

Each function should have one master management information system (MIS) from a single source, which can then be sliced with automation to provide the requisite information to authorized personnel. This will ensure that different groups do not get their information from different sources or in different formats.

It is important for a company to clearly assign responsibility to individuals or groups for producing these reports at specified intervals (daily, monthly, quarterly, etc.) and distributing them to pre-agreed recipients. For larger companies, what works best is to have a central team of experts to do this for all functions, using data emanating from pre-agreed sources, for example, the enterprise resource planning system for financial performance, network system, customer service software, human resource management system, etc., or even data from external sources such as the report of the Telecom Regulatory Authority of India (TRAI) giving quarterly revenues and revenue market shares of all operators.

These central teams are generally referred to as 'shared services group', 'central processing group', or 'central MIS department'. Having such a team would ensure that reports are not produced by concerned functions, and come straight from the system, thereby eliminating the possibility of doctoring reports to show better than actual performance.

The list of all reports, distribution lists based on designations and timelines need to be fixed, documented and carefully monitored. Distribution lists as per designations need to be linked to the human resource management system for automatic deletions and additions in case of changes in personnel or designations.

Distribution of such reports should be designed on the principle that at the lowest level, reports covering limited aspects, but with depth, are made available, and as the level of authority rises, the reports provided are broader in scope but limited in depth of detailing. As a result, at the topmost level, the report should cover all disciplines but only limited KRAs to provide a comprehensive and strategic view of the performance of each aspect of the business. This will ensure governance by exception as well as empowerment at all levels.

Quarterly audits and reporting—best example of corporate governance

I believe the best and most effective tool to ensure the accuracy and reliability of financial reports is quarterly full audits, which should be conducted by statutory auditors. Further, each quarter should be treated as a full year. Initially, it does seem like a daunting task and can be perceived to put undue pressure on the system, but once achieved, the practice becomes automatic. There can be no better and practical practice on corporate governance than this action (at Airtel and later at Infratel, we have been conducting full quarterly audits since 2002).

As already mentioned, I also firmly believe in a transparent quarterly comprehensive report on the financial as well as operational aspects of a company, available externally as well as internally (say on the company's website). The accountability of concerned persons and disciplines as a matter of process results in quick improvements and corrections. Our quarterly reports at Airtel and Infratel are much admired globally for their content, information and transparency.

It is well established that external stakeholders have greater respect for a company on account of transparency and disclosures. However, I believe that the real benefit of such reporting is internal, with clear accountability for shortcomings and corrective actions.

It must be ensured that for all performance measures, year-on-year comparisons as well as trends over the last few quarters are made available. Internally, the performance for the period (say a quarter) as well as year-to-date should also be seen vis-à-vis the agreed annual operating plan.

Accounting policies

One important aspect of transparent financial reporting is adopting accounting policies that mirror business requirements and realities. For example, in an industry with quick technological changes, depreciation policies with respect to such capex must reflect this reality by treating the life of machinery and equipment as relatively short and accordingly providing a higher depreciation charge as compared to a traditional industry where an asset's life will be longer due to fewer technological changes. Similarly, where extension of credit to customers is a norm, the accounting policy must make provisions to categorize as doubtful those outstanding payments that have not been made within a certain period from the due date—without exceptions. As an example of the outcome of not being disciplined in such matters, non-provision of loans given by our banks that are not being serviced by the borrower as per schedule—either by way of non-payment of interest or repayment of instalments in a timely manner (called non-performing assets or NPAs)—as doubtful of recovery due to laxity in rules and accounting policies in the Indian banking system has led to a serious problem with regard to NPAs. In other words, the accounting policies must be designed to ensure that no one can brush bad news or potential bad news under the carpet. It is better to reflect bad news early than to wake up too late, by which time it may be impossible to control the situation.

7

Treasury

'Whichever party is in office, the treasury is in power.'

—*Harold Wilson*

'Alexander Hamilton started the US Treasury with nothing, and that was the closest our country has ever been to being even.'

—*Will Rogers*

For everyone, ranging from individuals (including children getting pocket money) to families to small and medium businesses to large companies to state governments and municipalities to central governments and non-profit organizations, treasury management is an important function.

As companies become large, this assumes even more importance. Some common aspects to be managed by treasuries in all companies are given below.

Managing leverage

As discussed earlier in chapter six of Part I, a company must ensure that the overall debt taken by it is within reasonable and comfortable limits so that given its income, the company can easily service its debt, that is, pay periodic interest as well as pre-agreed repayment instalments well in time. This is popularly known as 'leveraging' and is generally measured as a multiple derived by dividing the total net debt (that is gross debt less cash and bank balances and investments that can be readily liquidated, such as fixed deposits, investments in mutual funds, etc.) by the company's EBITDA. In most companies, this leverage multiple should be kept below, say, three times EBITDA. In other words, the net debt of the company must not be more than three times its EBITDA to ensure timely payment of interest and repayments. If this ratio starts exceeding this level, the treasury must highlight the need to raise equity at the appropriate time and reduce debt with such proceeds. Conversely, if due to high free cash flow, leverage is likely to drop below the minimum desired levels (say at least 1x of EBITDA), the treasury should propose steps to distribute surplus cash to shareholders or invest excess cash in the expansion of the business. For good financial planning, a minimum level of debt is considered desirable to ensure a good balance between equity and debt. Some debt in the company ensures better financial discipline as the management has to ensure timely servicing of such debt.

Planning repayment schedules and keeping prepayment options

The treasury must ensure that debt repayment is planned in a spread-out, even and orderly manner and is not bunched up at unmanageable levels. Debt maturities and moratoriums on repayments need to be carefully planned to ensure this.

It should also be attempted that the terms of debt allow for prepayments as an option at period intervals (say on interest payment dates) without break fees, that is, penalties. This provides the flexibility to utilize extra cash flows or take advantage of refinancing (that is, replacing an existing loan with a new loan) at lower rates with falling interest rates in the market or a better credit rating of the company. Strong companies invariably manage this.

For this, the right balance may need to be maintained between bank financing (which normally would allow this flexibility) and market borrowings by way of bonds where such flexibility is difficult or costly to achieve. Prepayments to banks also ensure availability of lines of credit from such banks to the company for future requirements at quick notice.

Managing foreign exchange risk

For companies that are exposed to foreign exchange risk either in terms of imports or exports, especially in emerging markets where movements in exchange rates could be sudden, wide and volatile, foreign exchange management becomes crucial.

It is recommended that such companies lay down clear and unambiguous policies in this regard to maintain discipline and to curb the urge to indulge in speculation or take chances based on market predictions. The best of these predictions by some of the best-known pundits and institutions often go wrong by wide margins and thus it is better to be conservative and prudent in this regard. For instance, a policy providing that at any point of time the company shall ensure that of its total borrowings and payables at least say 70 per cent of exposure would have no open foreign exchange risk, that is, it is either in local currency or forward covers have been taken from banks against liabilities in foreign currency. A forward cover is like an insurance policy where the bank fixes the rate in local currency vis-à-vis the foreign currency being covered, against a forward premium (like an insurance charge) paid every year. As a result, the company no longer has to worry about fluctuations in foreign currency rates in future. Accordingly, the foreign currency liability against which forward cover is taken becomes akin to local currency liability. Such a policy ensures major risk mitigation while providing some flexibility to the treasury in deciding the extent of foreign currency exposure.

An effective and recommended principle on forward covers in the case of emerging markets where short-term volatilities in exchange rates can be lethal is to cover exposures in the shortest period to full and reduce the percentage of cover as the period of due dates increases. This would achieve the minimum prescribed percentage of cover most effectively. For instance, the treasury should decide to cover all foreign currency liabilities becoming payable in the next three months to 100 per cent, in the next three to six months to 75 per cent, in the next six to twelve months to 50 per cent and so on.

Reporting to ensure up-to-date knowledge of cash and bank balances and movements and net debt outstanding

An aspect that most companies ignore is the need to have a daily report showing actual status of cash and bank balances and debts with information on daily and month-to-date movements under broad heads. Companies that do not focus on treasury balances closely often run into trouble by not taking timely actions.

Other treasury reports

Similarly, periodic reports on other aspects of the treasury such as leverage ratios, servicing requirements in the near future, maturity profiles of loans, foreign exchange exposures, etc., at least on a monthly basis with preset formats and list of recipients is a must.

8

Internal Assurance

'We are all criminally insane, but most of us have good control mechanisms—internal and external. Remove the controls and you have a killer.'

—*Nelson DeMille*

One common malaise that I have noted across industries and companies is that internal assurance (referred to as internal audit in most companies) as a function is underrated and treated as a necessary evil imposed by statute.

Nothing could be further from the truth. In my experience—not as a chartered accountant or finance professional, but as a student of general management— internal assurance is one of the most critical functions in any organization and deserves the maximum attention by top management.

As you will have noted, I refer to this function as 'internal assurance' and not 'internal audit'. The reason is that I feel the scope of this function is beyond auditing the past and encompasses focusing on internal controls to ensure a smooth future.

I believe that to run any business, big or small, it is important to have robust internal controls, especially financial controls, to ensure:

1. Smooth operations by way of good processes;
2. That there is no scope for financial impropriety at any level of the organization;
3. Standardization of processes and rules across the organization, that is, knowledge management; and
4. That there is no repetition of an issue that may have arisen in any particular part of the organization across the entire organization.

Internal controls start with basic financial controls such as segregation of duties and delegation of authority to ensure that there is little (if not nil) chance of complicity and collusion amongst the different entities required to authorize a transaction. They extend to complex controls involving cybersecurity, IT and enterprise resource planning systems in operations, revenue assurance, data integrity, KYC verifications, forensics, human resource management solutions, network data integrity and availability of critical information online, followed by quick implementation.

A popular term currently in use, 'risk management', that is, countering or mitigating the risks facing an organization, is also a subset of internal controls. The comprehensive function encompassing risk management, internal audits to ensure implementation of processes and rules and internal controls is what I refer to as 'internal assurance'. As the term 'assurance' suggests, the ultimate purpose of this function is to assure senior management, the audit committee and the board that 'all is well'—a mantra immortalized by the hit Bollywood movie, *3 Idiots*. Just as the watchman chanting 'all is well' assures residents that they can sleep peacefully, the internal assurance function provides comfort that what is being reported is correct and that ample controls exist to prevent any (significant, at least) frauds in the organization.

Adopting certain practices can help ensure a robust internal assurance function. I have outlined these practices below.

An organization should conduct a quarterly full audit of accounts in all respects, including notes to accounts, which give relevant information on accounting policies adopted, details of major items appearing in P&L and balance sheets and other relevant observations or explanations on accounts. This is perhaps the most effective internal control tool that a company can introduce. At Bharti, we have followed it religiously since the listing of Airtel in 2002, with great results. I wholeheartedly recommend that this be adopted as a religion by every company wanting to assure stakeholders about the reliability of its financial reporting.

In addition to conducting a quarterly audit, it is important to ensure that every issue that comes to light in any part of an organization during an internal audit or otherwise is dealt with in two distinct ways:

1. As an 'incident solution' so as to plug the particular issue; and

2. As a systemic solution to ensure that the process to prevent such an occurrence is introduced across the organization.

Creating a 'scoreboard' of internal controls, particularly financial controls, based on a well thought out and externally ratified scoring methodology, will help monitor progress on this front and remove subjectivity or at least minimize it to say no more than 20 per cent of the overall score. This will ensure that the robustness of internal controls is based on objective and measurable facts and not on perceptions alone.

It is important to create a culture across the organization—starting from the lowest level right up to the top managers, audit committee and the board—to encourage internal controls at all levels and ensure that most routine activities are on 'autopilot' with strong protections (read controls) against malfunction.

Instead of basing successful implementation of internal controls on the assumption that the concerned persons will always follow the prescribed processes, it would be better to ensure that the IT system itself does not allow a transaction to proceed if controls/processes are not followed. This is usually a tough decision as initially things could slow down a bit with the rejection of proposed actions. However, once it is known that controls or established processes cannot be bypassed, compliance increases dramatically.

At Bharti, we have followed all of the above with conviction and discipline and the results have been very good, giving all of us the assurance that when we declare our quarterly results (duly audited) for operations spanning twenty countries, our controls and processes are functioning well and that everyone can rely on the reported results as being correct in all material aspects.

This is particularly important for young businesses with big sizes, such as e-commerce companies, which are trying to grow exponentially. In my experience, internal controls in such companies are by and large so weak that their reported results cannot be easily relied on. Due to such weak control, frauds and misappropriations are common and frequent.

It is my belief that the audit committee and the board of a company must play a vital role in inculcating this culture of controls across the organization by making these the focal points of attention themselves.

I would also recommend that while the internal team on assurance has to be of a very high quality and integrity, it is perhaps best to have an external audit firm conduct internal audits to ensure independence and minimize subjectivity.

9

Administration and Security

A visitor's first impression of an organization is formed by how orderly the reception and security are and how clean and hygienic the surroundings are. For instance, imagine the first impression of a visitor to a typical government office with rude and unkempt security guards, dirty and badly lit corridors, stained walls and staircases and dirty and smelly washrooms. It can only be a feeling of apprehension with regard to dealing with an inefficient and inconsiderate organization, irrespective of the merits and intelligence of the qualified IAS officers working there. On the other hand, a visitor to any reputed private company is likely to experience a courteous and efficient security staff and receptionists and a clean and hygienic environment with well-painted walls, polished furniture, shining floors and clean and hygienic washrooms. The immediate impression is bound to be of a caring and efficient organization that one would like to deal with.

Similarly, the employees working for an organization feel good about it and feel engaged if the organization takes care to look after their day-to-day requirements in an efficient and consistent manner.

As a result, every company must invest adequate effort and resources to ensure an efficient administration function, which should cover aspects such as:

1. Physical security (augmented by IT and cybersecurity)
2. General cleanliness and maintenance of facilities
3. Hygiene at the workplace including in terms of food served in the canteen to employees
4. Ensuring that employees and visitors are comfortable in every respect
5. Systems for efficient transportation, travel, etc., for employees
6. Food and beverage for staff and guests.

It is also imperative that to ensure the maintenance of high standards of the administrative and security functions, all concerned are encouraged to point out the shortcomings promptly and controls are introduced to ensure that corrective actions are taken quickly.

10

Investor Relations

In my experience, there are only a few companies with efficient and effective investor relations. I feel that Infosys, HDFC, L&T, Bharti Airtel and Bharti Infratel are amongst the few Indian companies that have robust investor relations with their transparent, reliable and regular quarterly reports that contain the necessary financial and operational information, as well as with their open and honest interactions with investors at regular intervals.

For every listed company, the investors need transparency and answers to their queries and concerns. Investor relations as a function is the bridge between the senior management of a company and investors and thus assumes great importance.

Investor relations can, however, only be as effective as the reporting that a company does to its investors periodically (quarterly in the case of India). A transparent report covering important financial and operational aspects that would be necessary for an analyst to analyse and project the future becomes an important tool for investor relations. Another benefit of a transparent report is that all members of the senior management team who interact with investors will be on the same page, thus ensuring consistency in messaging.

Having personally spent a significant amount of time interacting with investors over the past two decades, I would recommend the following guidelines for a listed company with respect to investor relations.

One should have regular but adequate and not excessive contact with investors. I would recommend participating in select investor conferences organized by leading banks in different parts of the world—say, four to five such conferences, for example, one in Singapore, one in Hong Kong and perhaps two in the US and one in London. These are always more efficient and productive than roadshows where a lot of time is wasted in shuttling between the offices of various investors.

The investor relations manager should be a reasonably senior person so that he/she can represent the company on his/her own and thereby shield the senior operating team members.

Further, the manager must generally stick to what is reported but have a thorough understanding of the contents of the reports and the reasons behind the results. This will enable the investor relations team to be consistent and non-discriminatory with a deep understanding of results and operations to deal effectively with investors and satisfy their queries.

An important imperative for the investor relations team is to listen carefully to the comments, feedback, queries and criticism from investors and relay them to senior management. Most investors are bright and experienced individuals who have seen and gone through various experiences and situations in different businesses. Their observations, queries, comments and suggestions need to be seriously considered as part of the strategy-forming exercise.

It is good practice to follow the quarterly reports with an investor call the following day to answer investor queries and concerns in a transparent manner. The call should be recorded and both the recording and the transcript should be posted on the company website.

Investor relations representatives must always be honest in their responses to investors' queries. It is better to say 'I do not know' rather than cooking up things or bluffing. The personal credibility of investor relations representatives matters a lot.

Investor relations team members must assist research analysts in preparing their reports. However, good companies do not try to influence an analyst to prepare reports that only show the company in a favourable light. It is important to respect the ability of an analyst to prepare a true and accurate report rather than respect him based on the report being favourable to the company. Good analysts need to be respected even if their reports are unfavourable.

In effect, investor relations personnel are the ambassadors of the company to the investors and other stakeholders on the one hand and on the other are the eyes and ears of the company to understand the concerns, criticisms and suggestions of the investors.

11

Legal and Secretarial

The legal and secretarial functions are generally treated as back-room functions by many organizations. To my mind, these two serve important purposes and thus need to be carefully planned, resourced and empowered for best results.

First, let us consider the secretarial function. Normally, this is the one that ensures compliance with various non-tax-related laws and the rules and guidelines laid down by the Companies Act, Securities and Exchange Board of India (for listed companies), Reserve Bank of India, Institute of Chartered Accounts and other relevant bodies and government agencies. Beyond this, good companies should treat the secretarial function as a guide and custodian for best-in-class corporate governance and transparency beyond the letter and truly in spirit. The responsibilities of the secretarial function would be to ensure that all policies and procedures with respect to corporate governance are duly followed, for example, conducting quarterly audits (if mandated by the board), approving all related party transactions by the audit committee, ensuring that the meeting of independent directors (without management presence) with auditors and amongst themselves takes place, including the ombudsman report for discussion at board meetings, ensuring that action taken reports on actions proposed by the board in earlier meetings are included in the board pack, and ensuring that relevant presentations include the issues and matters that the board has specified to be highlighted, etc.

The legal function has one important task in my view. It needs to promote a culture of simplicity in legal documentation so that any agreement can be understood by all concerned and not merely a legal expert. Different companies would have different strategies for the legal function, but I strongly feel that the most productive legal strategy is to be defensive and not excessively aggressive. The legal department should, to my mind, be encouraged to suggest win-win solutions and avoid litigation to the extent possible and as a culture.

However, in order to defend the organization it is imperative that the legal function has strong controls to ensure timely actions, a safe and efficient system of storage of documents in physical as well as digital form and finally, a strong MIS to ensure that important matters are duly pursued.

Since for most companies, legal matters would be to a large extent common for the entire industry, it should be ensured that the legal head is in regular contact with other industry players and industry associations to coordinate a common approach and strategy industry-wide on such issues. Whenever possible, the industry association should be encouraged to fight common legal battles on behalf of all members.

Besides a consistent stand and submissions, such an approach will save the fortunes being spent today in legal costs worldwide. I feel corporations need to make a concerted effort to significantly rationalize legal costs. One effective way would be to promote young legal talent and thus reduce the overdependence on a few top lawyers who are overworked (with little time for preparation) and who overcharge.

PART III

Activities and Norms That Comprise the 'Way of Working' of an Organization

Over the years, I have observed that there are certain activities that are common to all organizations, but each organization can have different ways of tackling them. In this section I discuss some of these everyday activities and offer my suggestions on dealing with them based on my experiences. I have no doubt that the logical handling of these activities can go a long way in making the organization efficient, productive and dependable, enabling it to respond quickly and systematically to changing or new situations.

1

Dealing with Competition and Competitors

'Competition has been shown to be useful upto a certain point and no further, but cooperation, which is the thing we must strive for today, begins where competition leaves off.'

—*Franklin D. Roosevelt*

'I have been up against tough competition all my life. I wouldn't know how to get along without it.'

—*Walt Disney*

I believe that in today's world, a major cause of the poor financial health of many industries across the globe is an inherent hatred for competitors (which many organizations make a part of their DNA and even take great pride in). That hatred—often fuelled by slogans like 'we will kill

the competition' or 'we shall make them surrender'—
invariably results in self-destruction as the company tries
to destroy the opposition. Such an attitude also brings out
the worst of human instincts with constant belittling of
competitors and running them down, even resorting to lies
and misrepresentations in doing so. Putting political and
other pressures from authorities on competing companies
is unfortunately being seen more often across geographies,
including but not limited to India.

I feel that if like human beings, corporations also adopt
the principles of mutual respect, ethics and consideration
for other competing companies, then the corporate world
(like the actual world) would be a better place.

In this world of intense competition, it is often seen
that competitors (even at individual levels) become and
behave more like enemies. A classic example of this, where
competitiveness is taken to ridiculous and childish levels,
is the rivalry between the employees of Coke and Pepsi. It
is well known that employees of one will never drink the
beverage of the other company, even if their own product
is not available.

As I have discussed earlier in this book, I am a
firm believer in competing and collaborating with the
competition. The formation of Indus Towers and the
philosophy behind tower companies is a prime example
of this and it had great results. With this in mind, I have a
few suggestions on how best to deal with competition and
competitors.

There must be mutual respect at both the individual
as well as corporate level. We need to remember that
our competitors and the people working for those
organizations are doing their job as diligently as we are

for our organization. Mutual respect and trust enables communication between competitors and it then becomes possible to point out bad practices being followed by the other that could severely harm the industry overall. For instance, if it comes to light that some employees of the competition are disposing of electronic waste in an unauthorized manner to non-certified buyers, it should be immediately pointed out since such an action can bring disrepute to the entire industry and subject all companies to investigations and harassment.

The most effective and efficient way to keep communication lines open and to discuss issues of mutual interest—for example, the stand best taken on common legal issues—is to create a platform in the form of an industry association with a full-time independent director general, where such healthy discussions can be taken up in a structured manner. General Mobile Systems Association (GSMA), which is a global association of mobile operators, is a great example of such interaction and collaboration. Joint efforts by competing operators under this body have resulted in unbelievable innovations that have improved the lives of millions of people across the globe. One outstanding example of such collaboration is from a few years back, when GSMA combined the volume commitments of most of its members to secure ultra-low-cost devices from global vendors. Such low-cost devices benefitted millions of low-income customers across the world by enabling them to avail of telecom services and thus enriching their lives. Bringing millions of customers on to telecom networks also promoted much-needed digitization and inclusive growth across the world, especially in underdeveloped and emerging economies.

It is a good practice to not only communicate concerns to the opposition but also genuine appreciation for a job well done, for example, an innovative product, a strong marketing/advertising campaign, leading the way in simplifying complexity or coming up with solutions to industry problems faced by all (say on legal action). One good example of this was in the Indian telecom industry where Jio introduced a few (less than ten) simple tariff plans in markets across India as against the hundreds of plans and sub-plans prevailing for other operators. The industry unanimously appreciated the much-desired simplification brought in by Jio, which helped others in streamlining their tariff plans.

It is my belief that mutual respect, trust and credibility amongst individuals on competing sides lead to creative and productive collaborations that go a long way in benefitting customers and ensuring the health of the industry.

2

Dealing with Vendors

'A smart manager will establish a culture of gratitude. Expand the appreciative attitude to suppliers, vendors, delivery people, and of course customers.'

—Harvey MacKay

'Technologies and specific vendors may come and go, but massive cultural transformations and new kinds of relationships? Those don't go away.'

—Clara Shih

Issues relating to supply chain management and the philosophy relating to relationships with vendors, that is, suppliers of equipment, goods or services, have been dealt with in different sections in this book (mainly under 'Business Delivery Model', chapter two of Part I).

In most companies (even in some of the best-known and celebrated ones), the principle aim of supply chain management is considered to be squeezing the maximum possible juice out of the vendors—big and small. In fact, it is seen as a company's natural right to squeeze the bigger vendors the most, with scant consideration given to their economics or the commitments made to them. The result is the tendency to constantly renegotiate even signed agreements in the name of protecting the interests of the organization. In addition, with a company having the power to make or break vendors, it often treats the vendor as a subject while the company is the king, or it regards the vendor as an enemy who is out to loot the company.

However, to my mind, it is clear that for the best results on a long-term sustainable basis, the way to deal with vendors of products and services is to work out win-win solutions.

Maintaining mutual respect, trust and credibility with vendors by being seen as a friend goes a long way in getting the best out of them. It is my belief that as the smallest player in the field initially, Airtel was able to become a leader because it was backed by dedicated vendors who we always treated as 'partners in progress' and who made our success their own goal. Our ability to make our partners trust us was the key. An effective way to develop mutual trust between the company and a vendor is to have regular sessions where future plans (to the extent they are not trade or strategic competitive secrets) are discussed. Invariably the inputs and suggestions made by vendors help in coming to the right decisions, besides promoting mutual trust and engagement.

I also believe that contrary to the general belief that vendors making healthy financial returns amount to adversity for the buyer, financially healthy and viable vendors are in the best interests of the buyer in the long run. This is so because only a healthy vendor can ensure quality, timely deliveries, innovation and ethics. He is also likely to stand with the buyer in periods of stress.

On the other hand, in my experience, if a vendor is pushed to the wall, he will invariably work out a way to extract the extra income—either by way of providing poor-quality goods or services, or by taking advantage of ambiguity in contracts. Unfortunately, because of a lack of trust, the reverse squeeze invariably happens when the buyer is under pressure and is dependent on the vendor.

One other aspect that ensures respect and loyalty from a vendor is fairness in dealings and timely payments, preferably without any reminders. Many companies feel proud when they are able to extract some extra credit period over the agreed period under some pretext or the other—often on account of 'quality issue' related delays. However, a company with an impeccable record of paying on time is always able to get concessions from vendors in the long run.

3

Annual Operating Plan or Budget Exercise

I have seen some of the most respected global companies spend a large part of the year and an unbelievable number of man hours in preparing an AOP or budget for the following year. I have discussed the basic philosophy behind AOPs in chapter four of Part I. I now offer some specific suggestions with regard to AOPs.

The basic purpose of an AOP is to assess the resources required to realize the potential for the next year(s) and plan for them well in advance. These could range from financing to human resources to technology and IT interventions or adding new activities/business segments. Line by line projections will not help in this. One needs projections on broad heads to assess the gaps. For instance, instead of struggling with fixing revenue targets for the year in terms of absolute amounts, it is easier to fix them as a percentage of total market revenue—say 35 per cent of the total market revenue. This would be easily acceptable vis-à-vis an absolute figure, which does not take into account possible positive or adverse developments in the market size. This is called a 'mark to market' approach.

AOPs are generally a big battle between the corporate office and operations with serious and at times bitter negotiations. I feel a simple way of avoiding this is to prepare a top-down AOP at the corporate office, independent of a bottom-up AOP prepared by the operating team. If the projections are within a certain percentage band of each other, the operating AOP should be adopted. The reason behind this is that the plan needs to be 'owned' by the operating team. It is natural for them to own their own proposed plan rather than a plan that is perceived to be thrust upon them. If projections are not within the percentage band, then areas of specific disconnect may be discussed in detail to understand the differences in thought processes and the reasons for misalignment. We have very successfully adopted this methodology at Bharti.

All AOPs must be prepared in full, that is, both P&L and balance sheet. Resource planning needs to be based on both and not just one of those. The reason is that P&L projections will determine the resources that need to be added to achieve, say, higher sales—for example, additional production capacities needed to cater to projected additional demand, more people or more outsourced activity partners, more retail points and therefore distributors, more office space and other administrative resources, addition of IT software, services and equipment. However, the projected balance sheet will show the additional resources in terms of funding required to achieve the P&L as per the AOP. Elaborate planning will be required to raise the necessary funding either by way of more equity, debt or vendor credits or combinations thereof. Obvious as it may sound, it is surprising that a majority of companies (including some very large companies) only finalize their AOPs for the P&L account. Not only that, many of them only plan till EBITDA.

Finally, I suggest opting for AOPs that the teams can achieve rather than chasing fantasies. Further, incentivize the team to beat the AOP. Pride in a team that beats an AOP is a magic potion for a passionate and vibrant company. Conversely, if despite their best efforts, teams find themselves falling short of targets, there can be nothing more lethal for destroying self-confidence, which in turn leads to pessimism and a general erosion of passion, energy and self-belief.

4

Governance Process

The success of an organization is directly correlated to the robustness and effectiveness of its governance. Governance, as described in earlier chapters, means reviewing and monitoring the operational performance in all respects at various levels of the organization. Good governance ensures accountability, early acknowledgement of shortcomings, appreciation of achievements, and taking prompt and clear corrective actions, wherever needed. I have provided below some specific suggestions in this regard that have been very effective for us at Bharti.

One should always strive to govern by exceptions. The key is to have a strong MIS whereby exceptional items— both positive and negative—are highlighted. Further, for governance at each level, starting with say the corporate office, reviews must be restricted to a handful of the most important KRAs, say ten at the most. Within these, time and energy should be conserved for 'outliers' on both the positive and negative side. Positive ones should be analysed to understand the actions or strategies resulting in exceptional positive results so that those learnings can be applied elsewhere. Negatives should be studied to understand the reasons for failures and to review what is not working. The aim has to be to find quick solutions with a focused approach to overcome the negatives as soon as possible. At each subsequent level of governance, the same approach should be followed with a few KRAs that are relevant for that review.

The periodicity of reviews conducted at the higher levels in the organization must reduce to give breathing space to operating teams. I feel that at most a monthly review should be done at the CEO's level, and periodicity could be relaxed in case of satisfactory performance—to say once a quarter.

It is important not to waste too many man hours in reviews. Only relevant persons should be present in the review meetings. Technology like video conferencing should be extensively used to include the relevant people located in distant geographies in the review. A lot of man hours and expenditure in travel can be saved this way.

Every governance meeting, that is, a meeting called to review the operational performance or specific aspects thereof, must identify the issues of concern, particularly those that recur often in an operation or in different operations. Governance will be useless if it does not provide decisions or directions for steps to be taken to find systemic solutions to recurring issues (so that they are dealt with once and for all as a process everywhere) and strategic decisions and directions for new issues facing the organization. The suggested rules for meetings, including governance meetings, are discussed in the following chapter.

All decisions as per the above must be recorded with specific responsibilities assigned to individuals with timelines, along with a process for monitoring progress.

5

Rules for Meetings

'I have left orders to be awakened at any time during national emergency even if I 'm in a cabinet meeting.'

—*Ronald Reagan*

'You should never go to a meeting or make a telephone call without a clear idea of what you are trying to achieve.'

—*Steve Jobs*

To obtain the best results, it is imperative to get the views of relevant people on any issue under consideration. Meetings to collectively discuss an issue with the concerned persons thus become a must. However, it is equally clear that in most companies, meetings are the biggest waste of man hours and are the cause of delayed actions because of 'inconclusive meetings'. It is often joked that the main aim of government meetings is to decide the time and venue for the next meeting on the same issue.

In order to make meetings effective and productive, I am suggesting a few rules (which I follow diligently with good results). Please note that while I am giving specific suggestions, these should be seen as guidelines that managers can tweak according to their own circumstances and style while (hopefully) retaining the spirit.

It is important to carefully select the attendees of a meeting. Only relevant people should be invited for the meeting, and they must be well prepared to answer any query relating to their area of responsibility (without being accompanied by a retinue of assistants). A golden rule is that the productivity of a meeting is inversely proportionate to the number of attendees. More the attendees, less are the chances of a productive meeting.

Along with deciding the attendees, it is important to ensure that they have all the relevant information required to make the meeting fruitful. Pre-reads help attendees prepare for a meeting and thus help make the meeting productive. They should be sent to all invitees, allowing them a reasonable amount of time (say at least forty-eight hours) to absorb the issues and frame questions. It is thus important that pre-reads be kept short and to the point. One should create a culture whereby attendees send their queries prior to the meeting so that the same can be effectively dealt with at least at the meeting, if not before. Also, those who have not read the pre-read should not be encouraged to participate in the meeting, as he/she may not be able to contribute much.

An important purpose of a meeting is to share information, and presentations, if used judiciously, are a valuable tool to achieve this. In order to ensure that the presentations made at meetings are effective, I suggest keeping in mind the following guidelines:

1. The presentation should be short—no more than twenty to twenty-five main slides with details in annexures, if required.
2. Use simple language that can be understood by all concerned.
3. Have clarity of thought and logical flow, giving the issue, the objective and the suggested solutions or actions.
4. Create a culture where substance over form is encouraged.

In addition to the above, a few other suggested rules for meetings are as follows:

1. Always specify the start and finish time of the meeting.
2. A meeting should not be longer than two hours.
3. A suggested format for meetings is provided below (say for 100 minutes):

    i. Summary (not the entire pre-read) to be presented in 10 minutes
    ii. Answers to queries in 20 minutes
    iii. Discussion on the issue and suggested possible actions in 40 minutes
    iv. Summary of the discussions

    - List agreed points
    - List disagreements   30 minutes
    - Next step(s) with timelines
    - Schedule next follow-up meeting

4. The minutes and a summary should be prepared after every meeting, and these should be circulated to all attendees within the next two days.

6

Developing Out-of-the-Box Thinking and Solutions

'Practice thinking outside the box, you will have plenty of time to think inside the box when you die.'

—*Testy McTesterson*

'Boxes are for objects, not humans.'

—*Abhijit Naskar*

In businesses where there is continuous evolution and change, it is important that the thinking and action plans also evolve to respond to the changing business environment. This is what is commonly referred to as 'out-of-the-box' thinking. It is called out-of-the-box because, typically, the corporate world is encased in boxes with set norms, processes and responses to situations based on what are perceived to be well-established and proven procedures.

People are generally discouraged from stepping out of the box into untried territory. I believe this is so because the majority of people are 'followers'. That is why the ratio of leaders (read entrepreneurs or entrepreneurial managers) to followers in the corporate world, as also in real life, is minuscule.

As India is a cricketing nation, perhaps a good example to illustrate the point is how players are trained. Coaches generally teach players to bat within the crease and not step out as that would carry the risk of being stumped if one missed the ball.

You would have noted that time and again, I have propagated the need for out-of-the-box and innovative thinking based on the principles of logic and simplicity. My personal and corporate experiences in this regard have been successful and satisfying. I now share with you some practices to promote such thinking.

Encourage the person wanting to put forth a new idea (however outlandish it may appear at first glance) to prepare what I call a 'concept note'. This note must clearly articulate the problem, the objective, the conventional approach and its problems, the approach suggested with pros and cons and suggested mitigations of such downsides or risks. The originator of the idea should give this concept note to his immediate boss, who should either take the discussion forward as per the suggestions given below, or provide an explanation to his boss as to why he does not deem it fit to pursue the concept. The higher authority in its discretion may decide to pursue the concept or drop it. Such a process will ensure that employees at all levels are encouraged to come up with innovative solutions and that their bosses cannot summarily reject them without assigning reasons.

The person who authorizes pursuing the concept should be responsible for selecting a small but relevant group that can add value to the concept.

The concept note should be circulated amongst the group members to get their views. However, general comments should be discouraged as those would already be part of the note. What is required is specific suggestions, along with areas of disagreement or new suggestions.

Once comments are received, the initiator may choose to incorporate some or all and modify his/her note.

The modified note should then be recirculated and a meeting called to debate the changes made as well as the changes suggested but not incorporated.

For best results, it is advisable to divide the participants into two groups representing opposing views with the senior-most member being neutral.

Following the debate, clear decisions should be taken, starting with whether to go ahead or drop the idea. If the decision is to go ahead with the idea, the group should agree on next steps and timelines.

To inculcate a culture of out-of-the-box thinking and innovation, I would recommend that the solutions agreed be named after the author and publicized across the organization.

All new solutions should be documented carefully so as to standardize and use them across the organization.

It is also important to file for intellectual property rights whenever deemed appropriate.

One important point to be kept in mind is that when encouraging innovation and fresh thinking, it is also made clear that people must not come up with frivolous proposals that are not backed by adequate research, contemplation and preparation to face any query or clarification sought.

I strongly believe that organizations which adopt this culture always remain ahead of the competition and times. The onus to encourage this and make it a way of life lies squarely with the top management.

For me, it has been a matter of great satisfaction and pride that since its inception, Bharti has been able to put out-of-the-box thinking into practice with some great results. The rapid and unimaginable scale-up that we achieved as a result of our approach to ideas like outsourcing, new ways of procurement and pricing, and our approach in deciding our business models, strategies and delivery models are very good examples of this thinking. These initiatives have been discussed in detail in chapter two of Part I of this book.

7

A Value-for-Money Culture

'Frugality includes all the other virtues.'

—*Cicero*

Most, if not all, large companies suffer from wastage in every field. The reason is that in absolute monetary or time terms such individual wastage does not matter vis-à-vis the overall scale and size of the company. The typical examples would be in travel. It is common in most companies that if three or four senior persons are travelling on the same flight and to the same hotel at the destination, there will invariably be a car arranged for each person because there is no system of coordination amongst the secretaries making the bookings. Such examples abound in large companies. The reason is the lack of a culture of 'value for money'. This is different from being stingy.

I am highlighting this aspect because once wastage becomes acceptable and the norm, it quickly seeps into all aspects of working and does not confine itself to small items.

Like the culture for innovation, the 'value for money' culture also needs to be led from the top.

A prime example of this culture is Azim Premji, founder of Wipro Ltd., one of the biggest IT companies in India. I vividly recall an incident that took place on the very day that Mr Premji was declared as the world's richest man in terms of personal wealth. That day he happened to come to our office to make a personal pitch for being selected as our prime IT partner. He was accompanied by a manager from Wipro's Delhi office and as the meeting ended, Sunil and I, out of courtesy and genuine respect for the man, came out to the portico of our office to see him off. We both expected a fleet of cars to transport him but were pleasantly surprised to see him stepping into the front seat of a Maruti 800, which was driven by his colleague from the Wipro office. It was indeed a humbling experience and one that instantly made my respect for Mr Premji go up by many notches.

I must, however, point out a potential danger in the excessive pursuance of value for money. It could result in a habit of cutting down on expenditure and investments that would be good for the organization in the medium to long term. A fine balance is an absolute must, otherwise there is always the danger of 'cutting the muscle along with the fat'.

8

The Speed versus Perfection Dilemma

'Have no fear of perfection—you never reach it.'

—*Salvador Dali*

'Perfection is the enemy of progress.'

—*Winston Churchill*

Every organization at every stage of evolution faces the dilemma of whether to pursue speed or perfection. It is indeed a debatable issue with supporters of both approaches. While it is true that vital time can be lost waiting for the elusive 'perfection', it is equally true that a shabby and poorly planned implementation in pursuit of 'speed' can be more of a disaster due to wasted efforts and losses or damages due to bad results.

To us at Bharti, the preference has always been for speed with a reasonably high level of preparation, to ensure that the effort does not boomerang. There is no point in delaying the project to wait for perfection. This approach is largely due to the clarity of thought on this aspect that Sunil had from day one that 'perfection can always be achieved as we move ahead, but an advantage lost because of slow speed of implementation can never be recouped'.

An apt example of this dilemma for Bharti was when we decided to go all India for mobile services after reasonable success in a few circles. While by then we had a good grasp on the fundamentals of running a good mobile operation (we had tie-ups with vendors, reasonably good major processes and information systems, and above all, we had arranged the required finances for new circles), we knew that we were far from being at par with established telecom operators globally in terms of quality and consistency of our services and overall controls—leave alone being perfect.

However, we opted for speed over perfection because the licences and spectrum were available at that time and may not have been available later. Speed certainly won and transformed Bharti into a large and coveted company. On the other hand, there are numerous instances where companies, in their wait for perfection, missed the bus. A prime example, as pointed out in chapter nine of Part III of this book, was a leading manufacturer of televisions in India which waited too long for the 'perfect' product by way of LED televisions and found itself becoming irrelevant in the market, which ultimately led to the company's closure.

Like most such dilemmas, the answer lies in balancing the two. Good organizations over time ensure quick action but after doing ample groundwork to ensure no major slippages and backlashes. Any such major shortcomings in the offering would obviously cause the product to be rejected, thereby negating the benefit of a quick launch.

Another practice that good companies follow (and which we at Bharti certainly do) is to systematically and unemotionally point out their own shortcomings with a clear mandate to fix them as soon as possible by way of a permanent solution to avoid recurrence.

9

Long-Term versus Medium-Term versus Short-Term Dilemma

'You can't grow long term if you can't eat short term.
Anybody can manage short
Anybody can manage long
Balancing those two things is what management is.'

—*Jack Welch*

Some organizations and managers believe in having very long-term planning and vision. Needless to say, this is a good approach, but I find two problems with it.

For one, a high percentage of organizations struggle to ensure their healthy survival in the short to medium term, leave alone in the long term.

Secondly, most industries have become so dynamic that a vision beyond a reasonable time frame has perhaps become meaningless.

I firmly maintain that every company has to first ensure success and financial health in the short and medium term (not more than three to four years). Once the ship stabilizes, one can gradually look towards the long term and make investments there against.

I have seen many companies fail because of their obsession with the long term, which clouded their short- and medium-term sight.

A classic example of this, as mentioned in the previous chapter, is a leading television company in India that decided that the future of the television industry was in LED and HD technology and accordingly refused to invest in technologies succeeding picture tubes like flat screens and plasma. The company, from an undisputed leadership position, simply ceased to exist as it took over a decade for LED and HD to become commercial realities.

There will be no long term if a company fails to get past the short and medium term. Secure those first.

Just as human beings need to survive and emerge healthy from childhood and then their teens to become healthy adults, a company needs to survive in the short term and gain strength and skills in the medium term to emerge as a robust and strong organization in the long run. A reverse approach of first trying to fix the long term is likely to result in infant mortality.

10

Dealing with Failure

'A man may fail many times but he isn't a failure until he begins to blame somebody else.'

—*John Burroughs*

'Do not judge me by my successes, judge me by how many times I fell down and got back up again.'

—*Nelson Mandela*

As we all know, everyone who tries something new does fail at times. The incident and frequency of failure increases for those people who try new things or ways not attempted before—in other words, those who dare to implement out-of-the-box solutions; a theme which has been strongly recommended in this book.

Just like it is important to remain grounded in success (like fixing things when they aren't broke—chapter 15 of

Part I), it is equally (and perhaps more) important to deal with failures.

To me, the biggest failure in dealing with failure is when one or both of the following happen:

1. Being in a state of denial over recognizing and accepting failure of a project or initiative.
2. Recognizing failure, but disowning the project that failed and shifting the blame on others, whether internally or externally.

As has been pointed out by virtually all successful leaders, irrespective of their fields, a failure that is well-handled can lead to great success.

I suggest a few rules an organization can follow to handle failure, learn from it and turn it into great success:

1. A decision to implement a project or agree on a particular action plan must necessarily be owned by each and every one who was part of the decision-making process. This 'collective ownership' is an absolute must, irrespective of whether one or more members of the decision-making team were not in favour of the decision or were in favour of a modified decision. Once a decision is made, it has to be a firm rule that each and every member 'owns' it.
2. 'Collective ownership' would ensure that there is no hesitation in acknowledging a failure. People try to hide a failure if the stigma of such failure gets attached to only a few individuals.
3. The next step is to build a culture of bringing the failure to everyone's notice as soon as possible. Delay

in identifying failure is the biggest reason for damage to organizations. Conversely, early detection and acknowledgement of a wrong decision will contain the damage in most cases.

4. The natural next step, if the fear of acknowledging failure is eliminated, is to undertake a 'root-cause analysis' of what led to the failure—again without assigning such specific causes to individuals and instead attributing them collectively to the entire team.

5. Once an honest and fearless assessment of the reasons for a failure is carried out, it becomes easy to learn from the mistake(s) and promptly take corrective actions (again with collective responsibility).

Organizations which do not promote 'collective responsibility' of failure and allow a culture of blame game and finger-pointing will inevitably fail.

One aspect which can make a leader great is when the team leader, while promoting the culture of 'collective responsibility', steps forward and takes the biggest blame of failure himself. Conversely, for every success, he must always be prepared to give the biggest credit to his team members and not to himself.

11

The Art of Scaling Up

'I am always amazed how overnight successes take a helluva long time.'

—Steve Jobs

It is my belief that unless a business or activity can be scaled up, there is no point in pursuing it.

As per my experience, scaling up a business is an art that needs to be carefully practiced. I share with you some suggestions in this regard.

To scale up, it is important to delegate. Delegating authority and responsibility ensures that more people take over and manage routine activities. This will leave the manager relinquishing those duties with the time to focus on creating scale. A good model is to separate tasks between the corporate office and operations. The corporate office should be responsible for finance, technology and seeking expertise, while operating teams and leaders need to be given the freedom to operate, but within specified boundaries.

While all resources can never be pre-planned in the scaling-up stage, one resource that must be fully planned to ensure a successful scale-up is finance. I feel that no project should be started without what is called 'financial closure', that is, completion of financial arrangements for the entire project. One has seen too many projects—great ones included—fail due to bad and inadequate financial planning. The real estate sector fiasco in India is a shining example of this. It is common knowledge that most real estate companies overstretched themselves financially by taking too much debt and by diverting funds received as advance in one project to be used as equity injection in the next project. In the process, many of them are today stuck with unfinished projects, which they could not complete due to their inability to service debt.

An important duty of the corporate or central office is to closely and effectively monitor progress, analyse data and take quick corrective actions. I would strongly recommend external expert help in the areas of project management and monitoring, especially in the early stages of a company. The reason why a company in the start-up stage should seek external expert help in designing its MIS and governance process is that a young company is unlikely to have such expertise in-house at a very early stage.

For a quick and successful scale-up, it is necessary that any issue or problem faced in any particular project is not allowed to recur elsewhere. For this, robust internal controls need to be introduced to ensure the introduction of suitable processes to overcome the problem and simultaneously implement them across the organization.

Finally, for scale-up, an organization must always be ready to evaluate organic versus inorganic growth, that is, by way of acquisitions or mergers. Sole reliance on organic growth could result in vital first-mover/early-mover advantage being lost, since setting up an operation (manufacturing or services) from ground zero involves a gestation period, which could vastly differ on a case-to-case basis. Acquisition of a running operation, on the other hand, would give the organization a head start and enable it to scale up the existing platform much faster. The choice would depend on costs involved, time gap between the two alternatives and competitive intensity in the market. For instance, assume a situation where a new product is introduced by a competitor, one that the company does not have, and one that is likely to require a long time to produce and test technically and in market. In such a situation, acquiring the company that has already developed that product and is available for acquisition at a reasonable valuation would be a better option to remain competitive.

We fortunately realized this early at Bharti by acquiring running mobile operations in Kolkata, Chennai, Karnataka, Andhra Pradesh, Rajasthan and the northeast and acquiring an existing licence in Punjab after the commencement of mobile operations organically in Delhi and Himachal Pradesh and fixed line in Madhya Pradesh.

Subsequently, we went on to an organic rollout of nine more mobile circles—four fixed-line circles, and national and international long-distance projects.

12

Negotiations

'Negotiation is often described as the art of letting the other side have your way. You have to give the other side a chance to put stuff on the table voluntarily.'

'As a negotiator you should strive for a reputation of being fair. Your reputation precedes you. Let it precede you in a way that paves success.'

—Christopher Voss

I have always been a big fan and follower of Sunil's philosophy on negotiations. He firmly believes that a good negotiation is one where at the end, both parties smile. If a negotiation results in one side rejoicing and the other crying, it is almost certain that the deal will be short-lived.

Building on this philosophy, I suggest a few rules to be applied when negotiating.

One has to believe in a win-win situation for all parties and accordingly every proposal or counter-proposal must be carefully tested to ensure that it is not one-sided but fairly balanced. In the corporate world, one deals with smart, experienced people. An attempt to push a proposal that is inherently one-sided will always be detected irrespective of one's best attempts to camouflage or sugar-coat it. A good way to test for fairness and balance in any proposal is to form two internal groups—one representing the company and the other representing the other side—and allow them to freely debate their viewpoints on various aspects of the proposal. The senior-most person must be the judge and remove such clauses or propositions that could be termed as one-sided and unfair to the other party.

The personal credibility of the people negotiating goes a long way in ensuring a successful deal. People who try to be cunning or dishonest under the guise of furthering the company's cause actually do the biggest disservice to their organization.

Communication must be clear and unambiguous, preferably by way of mark-ups wherever possible, so that there are no false expectations and misinterpretations.

In every long negotiation, there inevitably will be sessions that go badly with heated exchanges and accusations. To my mind, a good negotiator is one who can separate personal relations and equations and professional disagreements. One golden rule that I would strongly recommend and personally steadfastly follow is that irrespective of how heated the exchanges are, always end a session on a light and humorous note to signify a 'ceasefire' and resumption of personal respect and friendship.

Finally, never forget to send a note appreciating the intellect and fairness of the other side. That note will go a long way in establishing a lifelong personal relationship, trust and friendship.

I can say with confidence that this approach to negotiations never fails. We have followed it to the hilt at Bharti—especially in our earlier and formative stages. Every negotiation, whether with investors such as Warburg Pincus, Temasek, Qatar Foundation and many other large financial investors, or with financial intermediaries such as banks and financial institutions, or with strategic partners such as British Telecom Italia, SingTel or Vodafone, or with top vendors such as Ericsson, Nokia, Siemens, IBM and many more, followed this principle. The result is that even years after those deals, they all remember us as tough but fair negotiators and consistently recommend us to others.

13

Rules of Communication

'Half the world is composed of people who have something to say and can't and the other half who have nothing to say and keep on saying it.'

—Robert Frost

'The most important thing in communication is hearing what isn't said.'

—Peter F. Drucker

Communicating thoughts and information is an important activity for all human beings and this applies equally to corporations. The larger the organization, the more critical and significant does this aspect become. Good and clear communication can get everybody—internally and externally—on the same page and aligned. On the other hand, bad communication or lack of communication can create chaos and an atmosphere where rumours and misinformation and misinterpretation rule.

I share below a few suggestions for ensuring high-quality communication.

Transparency, clarity and simplicity in communication—whether internal or external—are key ingredients for effective and productive communication. Communication should also be structured, for example, following the quarterly results to explain the significant points to employees as well as investors and other stakeholders.

It is important to ensure consistency of message. To this end, it is generally good to post written communication, for example a news bulletin internally or a press release externally, which can form the basis for even verbal interactions.

It is good practice to assign a few spokespersons for such communication rather than have a free-for-all. This will also help shield other employees from a barrage of questions and queries.

Honesty is the key to good communication. If one does not want to share a particular piece of information, I suggest being honest and stating that the information cannot be shared for competitive reasons, for instance. Conversely, if one does not know the answer to a query, it is better to admit it and get back with an answer later, rather than bluffing or misinforming.

Communication should not be selective. Selectively providing information to a few chosen ones within a certain group—say amongst investors—can give rise to distortion of facts, misinterpretations, rumours being spread and also indicate favouritism. Giving some persons in a particular group information while withholding it from others in the same group can lead to dissatisfaction and heartburn. Even from a legal perspective, providing information to only a few investors can be a legal offence for listed companies. People responsible for communication must be clearly told not to indulge in this temptation with favourite journalists or investors. Discipline needs to be maintained in communication. A good practice is to put major interactions such as investor calls on the company website so that all that was stated becomes public information.

Finally, for all good organizations, a key element of the communication function is to quash rumours. Accordingly, if there are serious ongoing negotiations for a deal, it would be good to try and put such endeavours in the public domain as soon as possible with disclaimers that these discussions may or may not result in any transaction or agreement. Till then a golden statement generally is 'we do not as a principle comment on speculation'.

All the above principles and suggestions apply equally irrespective of the communication being with outsiders or within the company—be it from the CEO to all employees, between a manager and his team or between peers.

The need for responsible communication on the lines suggested above has perhaps never been more than in this age of social media where news and fake news, rumours, perceptions and outbursts can spread faster than any dreaded epidemic. The only way to counter these is for the company to communicate honestly, transparently and without discrimination.

Acknowledgements

I had a vague desire for quite some time to write about the experience and knowledge I have gained in my professional life—especially in the last twenty-five years at Bharti—with the intent and hope that some of it could be useful to other managers and to students aspiring to be managers.

A lot of my colleagues at Bharti—some who are still with Bharti and many who left at different points—encouraged me to pursue this desire and write a book encompassing my learnings. My family—my wife, Archana, and my children, Avantika and Anubhav—relentlessly reminded me to do so too. In addition, some of my close friends backed the idea strongly and gave me the encouragement to proceed. My deep gratitude to all of them—without their encouragement and persistence I might not have had the energy to pen this book.

However, funnily, it was an accidental meeting with Radhika Marwah of Penguin Random House India and a colleague of hers a couple of years back in Jaipur when

Archana and I accidentally walked into a party organized by them instead of another dinner elsewhere in Rambagh Palace, where we were to actually go, which brought serious shape to this effort. Radhika encouraged me to write a book on my years and experiences at Bharti, which I declined because I firmly believe that the incredible Bharti story must be penned only by Sunil. In the course of our conversation, I discussed with them the theme that I had in mind (the theme of this book), to share my thoughts on management, which they felt was a good idea and encouraged me to pursue it. My sincere thanks to them for encouraging me and a special thanks to Radhika for guiding me at every stage, editing the manuscript and suggesting some additions from time to time. In fact, to some extent, I did have to compromise my style of being direct, to the point and short at her behest as she felt that for the benefit of the readers, several chapters needed some more background and more examples.

Due to time constraints, it has taken me over two years to complete this book. But for the long and frequent international flights that provided me with the time as well as the solitude to focus my thoughts, there is no way that this book could have been completed. Also, many thanks to my executive assistant, T.V. Rajesh, who spent a lot of his time after office hours typing the manuscript and amending it several times.

I do hope that this book serves some useful purpose by being of help to aspiring managers and leaders in the business world and does not merely fulfil my own desire of penning my thoughts and experiences.

I would like to dedicate this book to all my colleagues at Bharti led by Sunil who helped me learn at every step.

They mentored and supported me in giving practical shape to several of my ideas, most of which were unconventional, untried and without precedent. Many of them reflected the contrarian view vis-à-vis established norms. My sincere thanks to all of them for giving me immense professional satisfaction and the privilege of working with them over the years.